Ants and Some Other Insects

An Inquiry into

The Psychic Powers of these Animals

With an Appendix on

The Peculiarities of Their Olfactory Sense

By

Dr. August Forel
Late Professor of Psychiatry at the University of Zurich

Translated from the German

By

Prof. William Morton Wheeler
American Museum of Natural History, New York

ISBN: 979-8-89096-033-7

Printed: March 2023

Published and Distributed By:
Lushena Books
607 Country Club Drive, Unit E
Bensenville, IL 60106
www.lushenabks.com

ISBN: 979-8-89096-033-7

ANTS AND SOME OTHER INSECTS.

WHEN discussing the ant-mind, we must consider that these small animals, on the one hand, differ very widely from ourselves in organisation, but on the other hand, have come, through so-called convergence, to possess in the form of a social commonwealth a peculiar relationship to us. My subject, however, requires the discussion of so many complicated questions that I am compelled to assume acquaintance with the work of others, especially the elements of psychology, and in addition the works of P. Huber, Wasmann, von Buttel-Reepen, Darwin, Romanes, Lubbock, my *Fourmis de la Suisse*, and many others. Since the functions of the sense-organs constitute the basis of comparative psychology, I must also refer to a series of articles entitled "Sensations des Insectes" which I have recently published (1900–1901) in the *Rivista de Biologia Generale*, edited by Dr. P. Celesia. In these papers I have defined my position with respect to various authors, especially Plateau and Bethe.

Very recently Bethe, Uexkull, and others have denied the existence of psychic powers in invertebrate animals. They explain the latter as reflex-machines, and take their stand on the ground of the so-called psycho-physical parallelism for the purpose of demonstrating our inability to recognise mental qualities in these animals. They believe, however, that they can prove the mechanical regularity of behavior, but assume unknown forces whenever they are left in the lurch in their explanations. They regard the mind as first making its appearance in the vertebrates, whereas the old Cartesians regarded all animals, in contradistinction to man, as mindless (unconscious) machines.

The Jesuit father E. Wasmann and von Buttel-Reepen are willing, on the other hand, to accept the inductive inference from analogy as a valid scientific method. Like Lubbock, the lecturer and others, they advocate a comparative psychology of the invertebrates and convincingly demonstrate the existence of psychic faculties in these animals. Wasmann, however, puts a very low estimate on the mental powers of the higher vertebrates and, in my opinion, improperly, denies to them any ability of drawing inferences from experience when in the presence of new conditions (this alone he designates as intelligence); he believes that man alone possesses an immortal soul (independent of natural laws?) in addition to the animal mind.

It is necessary, first of all, to arrive at some common understanding concerning the obscure notion "psychic" in order that we may avoid logomachy, and carrying on theology in the sense of Goethe's Mephistopheles. Two concepts are confounded in an obscure manner in the word "psychic": first, the abstract concept of introspection, or subjectivism, i. e., observation from within, which every person knows only, and can know only, in and by himself. For this let us reserve the term "consciousness." Second, the "activity" of the mind or that which determines the contents of the field of consciousness. This has been included without further ado with consciousness in the wider sense, and thence has arisen the confusion of regarding consciousness as an attribute of the mind. In another place I have designated the molecular wave of activity of the neural elements as "neurocyme."

We cannot speak of the consciousness of human beings other than ourselves without drawing an inference from analogy; quite as little ought we to speak of a consciousness of forgotten things. The field of our consciousness is constantly changing. Things appear in it and disappear from it. Memory, through association, enables us to recall, more or less directly and with more or less difficulty, things which appear to be momentarily absent from consciousness. Moreover, both the experience of self-observation and the phenomena of hypnotism teach us experimentally that many things of which we seem to be unconscious, are nevertheless present in consciousness or have been.   Indeed, certain sense-impressions remain, at the moment of their occurrence, unconscious so far as our ordinary consciousness or superconsciousness is concerned, although they can be subsequently recalled into consciousness by suggestion.   Whole chains of brain-activities, (dreams, somnambulism, or secondary consciousness) seem ordinarily to be excluded from the superconsciousness, but may subsequently be associated by suggestion with the remembered contents of consciousness.   In all these cases, therefore, what seems to be unconscious is after all proved to be conscious.   The above-mentioned phenomena have frequently led to mystical interpretations, but they are explainable on a very simple assumption.   Let us assume —and this is quite in harmony with observation—that the fields of the introspectively conscious brain-activities are limited by so-called association or dissociation processes, i. e., that we are unable actively to bring them all into connection at the same time, and that therefore all that seems to us unconscious has also in reality a consciousness, in other words, a subjective reflex, then the following results: Our ordinary waking consciousness or superconsciousness is merely an inner subjective reflex of those activities of attention which are most intimately connected with one another, i. e., of the more intensively concentrated maxima of our cerebral activities during waking.   There exist, however, other consciousnesses, partly forgotten, partly only loosely or indirectly connected with the contents of the superconsciousness, in contradistinction to which these may be designated as subconsciousness.   They correspond to other less concentrated or otherwise associated cerebral activities.   We are bound to assume the existence of still more remotely interconnected subconsciousnesses for the infra-cortical (lower) brain-centers, and so on.

It is easy to establish the fact that the maximum of our psychic activity, namely, attention, passes every moment from one perception or thought to another.   These objects of attention, as visual or auditory images, will-impulses, feelings or abstract thoughts, come into play—and of this there is no doubt—in different brain-regions or neuron-complexes.   We can therefore compare attention

to a functional *macula lutea* wandering in the brain, or with a wandering maximal intensity of neurocymic activity.   But it is quite as
satisfactorily established that other psychic phenomena external to
attention are likewise present in consciousness, though in a feebler
condition.   Finally, it is well known that all that has been in consciousness—even that which is now more, now less, forgotten—is
included in the psychic, i. e., in the contents of consciousness.   On
superficial consideration this appears to satisfy theoretical require-
ments.   But in fact and in truth there are innumerable processes
of which we are feebly conscious for only a scarcely appreciable
instant and which anon disappear from consciousness.   Here and
not in the strong and repeated "psychomes"—I beg your indulgence for this word, with which I would for the sake of brevity
designate each and every psychic unit—are we to seek the transi-
tion from the conscious to the apparently unconscious.   Even in
this case, however, the feeble condition of consciousness is only
apparent, because the inner reflex of these processes can merely
echo faintly in the field of a strongly diverted attention.   This,
therefore, in no wise proves that such half conscious processes are
in and for themselves so feebly represented in consciousness, since
a flash of attention is sufficient subsequently to give them definite
shape in consciousness.   Only in consequence of the diversion of
the attention do they lose more and more their connection with the
chain of intensity-maxima which, under ordinary circumstances,
constitute the remembered contents of our superconsciousness.
The more feebly, however, they are bound to the latter, with the
more difficulty are such half-conscious processes later associated
anew through memory with the dominant chain.   Of such a nature
are all dreams, all the subordinate circumstances of our lives, all
automatised habits, all instincts.   But if there exists between the
clearly conscious and the unconscious, a half-conscious brain-life,
whose consciousness appears to us so feeble merely on account of
the deviation of our ordinary train of memories, this is an unequivocal indication that a step further on the remaining connection
would be completely severed, so that we should no longer have the
right to say that the brain-activities thus fading away nebulously

• from our superconsciousness do not have consciousness in and for themselves. For the sake of brevity and simplicity we will ascribe subconsciousness to these so-called unconscious brain-processes.

If this assumption is correct—and all things point in this direction—we are not further concerned with consciousness. It does not at all exist as such, but only through the brain-activity of which it is the inner reflex. With the disappearance of this activity, consciousness disappears. When the one is complicated, the other, too, is complicated. When the one is simple, the other is correspondingly simple. If the brain-activity be dissociated, consciousness also becomes dissociated. Consciousness is only an abstract concept, which loses all its substance with the falling away of "conscious" brain-activity. The brain-activity reflected in the mirror of consciousness appears therein subjectively as a summary synthesis, and the synthetical summation grows with the higher complications and abstractions acquired through habit and practice, so that details previously conscious (e. g., those involved in the act of reading) later become subconscious, and the whole takes on the semblance of a psychical unit.

Psychology, therefore, cannot restrict itself merely to a study of the phenomena of our superconsciousness by means of introspection, for the science would be impossible under such circumstances. Everybody would have only his own subjective psychology, after the manner of the old scholastic spiritualists, and would therefore be compelled to doubt the very existence of the external world and his fellow-men. Inference from analogy, scientific induction, the comparison of the experiences of our five senses, prove to us the existence of the outer world, our fellow-men and the psychology of the latter. They also prove to us that there is such a thing as comparative psychology, a psychology of animals. Finally our own psychology, without reference to our brain-activity, is an incomprehensible patchwork full of contradictions, a patchwork which above all things seems to contradict the law of the conservation of energy.

It follows, furthermore, from these really very simple reflections that a psychology that would ignore brain-activity, is a monstrous

impossibility. The contents of our superconsciousness are con- •
tinually influenced and conditioned by subconscious brain-activities. Without these latter it can never be understood. On the
other hand, we understand the full value and the ground of the
complex organisation of our brain only when we observe it in the
inner light of consciousness, and when this observation is supple-
mented by a comparison of the consciousness of our fellow-men as
this is rendered possible for us through spoken and written language by means of very detailed inferences from analogy. The
mind must therefore be studied simultaneously from within and
from without. Outside ourselves the mind can, to be sure, be
studied only through analogy, but we are compelled to make use of
this the only method which we possess.

Some one has said that language was given to man not so
much for the expression as for the concealment of his thoughts. It
is also well known that different men in all honesty attribute very
different meanings to the same words. A savant, an artist, a
peasant, a woman, a wild Wedda from Ceylon, interpret the same
words very differently. Even the same individual interprets them
differently according to his moods and their context. Hence it
follows that to the psychologist and especially to the psychiatrist—
and as such I am here speaking—the mimetic expression, glances
and acts of a man often betray his true inner being better than his
spoken language. Hence also the attitudes and behavior of animals have for us the value of a "language," the psychological importance of which must not be underestimated. Moreover, the
anatomy, physiology and pathology of the animal and human brain
have yielded irrefutable proof that our mental faculties depend on
the quality, quantity, and integrity of the living brain and are one
with the same. It is just as impossible that there should exist a
human brain without a mind, as a mind without a brain, and to
every normal or pathological change in the mental activity, there
corresponds a normal or pathological change of the neurocymic activity of the brain, i. e., of its nervous elements. Hence what we
perceive introspectively in consciousness is cerebral activity.

As regards the relation of pure psychology (introspection) to the physiology of the brain (observation of brain-activity from with-out), we shall take the theory of identity for granted so long as it is in harmony with the facts. The word identity, or monism, im-plies that every psychic phenomenon is the same real thing as the molecular or neurocymic activity of the brain-cortex coinciding with it, but that this may be viewed from two standpoints. The phenomenon alone is dualistic, the thing itself is monistic. If this were otherwise there would result from the accession of the purely psychical to the physical, or cerebral, an excess of energy which would necessarily contradict the law of the conservation of energy. Such a contradiction, however, has never been demonstrated and would hold up to derision all scientific experience. In the mani-festations of our brain-life, wonderful as they undoubtedly are, there is absolutely nothing which contradicts natural laws and jus-tifies us in postulating the existence of a mythical, supernatural "psyche."

On this account I speak of monistic identity and not of psycho-physical parallelism. A thing cannot be parallel with itself. Of course, psychologists of the modern school, when they make use of this term, desire merely to designate a supposed parallelism of phenomena without prejudice either to monism or dualism. Since, however, many central nervous processes are accessible neither to physiological nor to psychological observation, the phenomena ac-cessible to us through these two methods of investigation are not in the least parallel, but separated from one another very unequally by intermediate processes. Moreover, inasmuch as the dualistic hypothesis is scientifically untenable, it is altogether proper to start out from the hypothesis of identity.

It is as clear as day that the same activity in the nervous sys-tem of an animal, or even in my own nervous system, observed by myself, first by means of physiological methods from without, and second, as reflecting itself in my consciousness, must appear to me to be totally different, and it would indeed be labor lost to try to convert the physiological into psychological qualities or *vice versa*. We cannot even convert one psychological quality into another, so far as the reality symbolised by both is concerned ; e. g., the tone, the visual and tactile sensation, which a uniform, low, tuning-fork vibration produces on our three corresponding senses. Nevertheless, we may infer inductively that it is the same reality, the same vibration which is symbolised for us in these three qualitatively and totally different modes; i. e., produces in us these three different psychical impressions which cannot be transformed into one another. These impressions depend on activities in different parts of the brain and are, of course, as such actually different from one another in the brain. We speak of psycho-physiological identity only when we mean, on the one hand, the cortical neurocyme which directly conditions the conscious phenomena known to us, on the other hand, the corresponding phenomena of consciousness.

And, in fact, a mind conceived as dualistic could only be devoid of energy or energy-containing. If it be conceived as devoid of energy (Wasmann), i. e., independent of the laws of energy, we have arrived at a belief in the miraculous, a belief which countenances the interference with and arbitrary suspension of the laws of nature. If it be conceived as energy-containing, one is merely playing upon words, for a mind which obeys the law of energy is only a portion of the cerebral activities arbitrarily severed from its connections and dubbed "psychic essence," only that this may be forthwith discredited. Energy can only be transformed qualitatively, not quantitatively. A mind conceived as dualistic, if supposed to obey the law of energy, would have to be transformed completely into some other form of energy. But then it would no longer be dualistic, i. e., no longer essentially different from the brain-activities.

Bethe, Uexkull, and others would require us to hold fast to the physiological method, because it alone is exact and restricts itself to what can be weighed and measured. This, too, is an error which has been refuted from time immemorial. Only pure mathematies is exact, because in its operations it makes use solely of equations of abstract numbers. The concrete natural sciences can never be exact and are as unable to subsist without the inductive method of inference from analogy as a tree without its roots. Bethe and Uexkull do not seem to know that knowledge is merely relative. They demand absolute exactitude and cannot understand that such a thing is impossible. Besides, physiology has no reason to pride itself upon the peculiar exactitude of its methods and results.

Although we know that our whole psychology appears as the activity of our cerebrum in connection with the activities of more subordinate nerve-centers, the senses and the muscles, nevertheless for didactic purposes it may be divided into the psychology of cognition, of feeling and volition. Relatively speaking, this subdivision has an anatomico-physiological basis. Cognition depends, in the first instance, on the elaboration of sense-impressions by the brain; the will represents the psycho- or-cerebrofugal resultants of cognition and the feelings together with their final transmission to the muscles. The feelings represent general conditions of excitation of a central nature united with elements of cognition and with cerebrofugal impulses, which are relatively differentiated and refined by the former, but have profound hereditary and phylogenetic origins and are relatively independent. There is a continual interaction of these three groups of brain-activities upon one another. Sense-impressions arouse the attention; this necessitates movements; the latter produce new sense-impressions and call for an active selection among themselves. Both occasion feelings of pleasure and pain and these again call forth movements of defense, flight, or desire, and bring about fresh sense-impressions, etc. Anatomically, at least, the sensory pathways to the brain and their cortical centers are sharply separated from the centers belonging to the volitional pathways to the muscles. Further on in the cerebrum, however, all three regions merge together in many neurons of the cortex.

Within ourselves, moreover, we are able to observe in the three above-mentioned regions all varieties and degrees of so-called psychic dignity, from the simplest reflex to the highest mental manifestations. The feelings and impulses connected with self-preservation (hunger, thirst, fear) and with reproduction (sexual love and its concomitants) represent within us the region of long-inherited, profoundly phyletic, fixed, instinct-life. These instincts are nevertheless partially modified and partly kept within due bounds through the interference of the higher cerebral activities. The enormous mass of brain-substance, which in man stands in no direct relation to the senses and musculature, admits not only of an enormous storing up of impressions and of an infinite variety of motor innervations, but above all, of prodigious combinations of these energies among themselves through their reciprocal activities and the awakening of old, so-called memory images through the agency of new impressions. In contradistinction to the compulsory, regular activities of the profoundly phyletic automatisms, I have used the term "plastic" to designate those combinations and individual adaptations which depend on actual interaction in the activities of the cerebrum. Its loftiest and finest expression is the plastic imagination, both in the province of cognition and in the province of feeling, or in both combined. In the province of the will the finest plastic adaptability, wedded to perseverance and firmness, and especially when united with the imagination, yields that loftiest mental condition which gradually brings to a conclusion during the course of many years decisions that have been long and carefully planned and deeply contemplated. Hence the plastic gift of combination peculiar to genius ranks much higher than any simpler plastic adaptability.

The distinction between automatism and plasticity in brain-activity is, however, only a relative one and one of degree. In the most different instincts which we are able to influence through our cerebrum, i. e., more or less voluntarily, like deglutition, respiration, eating, drinking, the sexual impulse, maternal affection, jealousy, we observe gradations between compulsory heredity and plastic adaptability, yes, even great individual fluctuations according to the intensity of the corresponding hereditary predispositions.

Now it is indisputable that the individual Pithecanthropus or allied being, whose cerebrum was large enough gradually to construct from onomatopœas, interjections and the like, the elements of articulate speech, must thereby have acquired a potent means of exploiting his brain. Man first fully acquired this power through written language. Both developed the abstract concept symbolised by words, as a higher stage in generalisation. All these things give man a colossal advantage, since he is thereby enabled to stand on the shoulders of the written encyclopædia of his predecessors. This is lacking in all animals living at the present time. Hence, if we would compare the human mind with the animal mind, we must turn, not to the poet or the savant, but to the Wedda or at any rate to the illiterate. These people, like children and animals, are very simple and extremely concrete in their thinking. The fact that it is impossible to teach a chimpanzee brain the symbols of language proves only that it is not sufficiently developed for this purpose. But the rudiments are present nevertheless. Of course the "language" of parrots is no language, since it symbolises nothing. On the other hand, some animals possess phyletic, i. e., hereditarily and instinctively fixed cries and gesture, which are as instinctively understood. Such instinctive animal languages are also very widely distributed and highly developed among insects, and have been fixed by heredity for each species. Finally it is possible to develop by training in higher animals a certain mimetic and acoustic conventional language-symbolism, by utilising for this purpose the peculiar dispositions of such species. Thus it is possible to teach a dog to react in a particular manner to certain sounds or signs, but it is impossible to teach a fish or an ant these things. The dog comprehends the sign, not, of course, with the reflections of human understanding, but with the capacity of a dog's brain. And it is, to be sure, even more impossible to teach its young an accomplishment so lofty for its own brain as one which had to be acquired by training, than for the Wedda or even the negro to transmit his acquired culture by his own impulse. Even the impulse to do this is entirely lacking. Nevertheless, every brain that is trained by man is capable of learning and profiting much from the experience of its own individual life. And one discovers on closer examination that even lower animals may become accustomed to some extent to one thing or another, and hence trained, although this does not amount to an understanding of conventional symbols.

In general we may say, therefore, that the central nervous system operates in two ways: *automatically* and *plastically*.

The so-called reflexes and their temporary, purposefully adaptive, but hereditarily stereotyped combinations, which respond always more or less in the same manner to the same stimuli, constitute the paradigm of automatic activities. These have the deceptive appearance of a "machine" owing to the regularity of their operations. But a machine which maintains, constructs, and reproduces itself is not a machine. In order to build such a machine we should have to possess the key of life, i. e., the understanding of the supposed, but by no means demonstrated, mechanics of living protoplasm. Everything points to the conclusion that the instinctive automatisms have been gradually acquired and hereditarily fixed by natural selection and other factors of inheritance. But there are also secondary automatisms or habits which arise through the frequent repetition of plastic activities and are therefore especially characteristic of man's enormous brain-development.

In all the psychic provinces of intellect, feeling, and will, habits follow the constant law of perfection through repetition. Through practice every repeated plastic brain-activity gradually becomes automatic, becomes "second nature," i. e., similar to instinct. Nevertheless instinct is not inherited habit, but phylogenetically inherited intelligence which has gradually become adapted and crystalised by natural selection or by some other means.

Plastic activity manifests itself, in general, in the ability of the nervous system to conform or adapt itself to new and unexpected conditions and also through its faculty of bringing about internally new combinations of neurocyme. Bethe calls this the power of modification. But since, notwithstanding his pretended issue with anthropomorphism, he himself continually proceeds in an anthropomorphic spirit and demands human ratiocination of animals, if they are to be credited with plasticity (power of modification),—he naturally overlooks the fact that the beginnings of plasticity are primordial, that they are in fact already present in the Amœba, which adapts itself to its environment. Nor is this fact to be conjured out of the world by Loeb's word "tropisms."

Automatic and plastic activities, whether simple or complex, are merely relative antitheses. They grade over into each other,

e. g., in the formation of habits but also in instincts. In their extreme forms they resemble two terminal branches of a tree, but they may lead to similar results through so-called convergence of the conditions of life (slavery and cattle-keeping among ants and men). The automatic may be more easily derived from the plastic activities than *vice versa.* One thing is established, however: since a tolerably complicated plastic activity admits of many possibilities of adaptation in the individual brain, it requires much more nervous substance, many more neurons, but has more resistances to overcome in order to attain a complicated result. The activities of an Amœba belong therefore rather to the plasticity of living molecules, but not as yet to that of coöperating nerve-elements; as cell-plasticity it should really be designated as "undifferentiated."[1] There are formed in certain animals specially complex automatisms, or instincts, which require relatively little plasticity and few neurons. In others, on the contrary, there remains relatively considerable nerve-substance for individual plasticity, while the instincts are less complicated. Other animals, again, have little besides the lower reflex centers and are extremely poor in both kinds of complex activities. Still others, finally, are rich in both. Strong so-called "hereditary predispositions" or unfinished instincts constitute the phylogenetic transitions between both kinds of activity and are of extraordinarily high development in man.

Spoken and especially written language, moreover, enable man to exploit his brain to a wonderful extent. This leads us to underestimate animals. Both in animals and man the true value of the brain is falsified by training, i. e., artificially heightened. We overestimate the powers of the educated negro and the trained dog and underestimate the powers of the illiterate individual and the wild animal.

I beg your indulgence for this lengthy introduction to my sub-

---

[1] If I expressly refrain from accepting the premature and unjustifiable identification of cell-life with a "machine," I nevertheless do not share the so-called vitalistic views. It is quite possible that science may sometime be able to produce living protoplasm from inorganic matter. The vital forces have undoubtedly originated from physico-chemical forces. But the ultimate nature of the latter and of the assumed material atoms is, of course, metaphysical, i. e., unknowable.

ject, but it seemed necessary that we should come to some understanding concerning the validity of comparative psychology. My
further task now consists in demonstrating to you what manner of
psychical faculties may be detected in insects. Of course, I shall
select in the first place the ants as the insects with which I am
most familiar. Let us first examine the brain of these animals.

In order to determine the psychical value of a central nervous
system it is necessary, first, to eliminate all the nerve-centers which
subserve the lower functions, above the immediate innervation of
the muscles and sense-organs as first centers. The volume of such
neuron-complexes does not depend on the intricacy of mental work
but on the number of muscle-fibres concerned in it, the sensory
surfaces, and the reflex apparatus, hence above all things on the
size of the animals. Complex instincts already require the inter-
vention of much more plastic work and for this purpose such nerve-
centers alone would be inadequate.

A beautiful example of the fact that complex mental combinations require a large nerve-center dominating the sensory and mus-
cular centers is furnished by the brain of the ant. The ant-colony
commonly consists of three kinds of individuals: the queen, or
female (largest), the workers which are smaller, and the males
which are usually larger than the workers. The workers excel in
complex instincts and in clearly demonstrable mental powers
(memory, plasticity, etc.). These are much less developed in the
queens. The males are incredibly stupid, unable to distinguish
friends from enemies and incapable of finding their way back to
their nest. Nevertheless the latter have very highly developed
eyes and antennae, i. e., the two sense-organs which alone are connected with the brain, or supra-oesophageal ganglion and enable
them to possess themselves of the females during the nuptial flight.
No muscles are innervated by the supra-oesophageal ganglion.
These conditions greatly facilitate the comparison of the perceptive organs, i. e., of the brain (*corpora pedunculata*) in the three
sexes. This is very large in the worker, much smaller in the female, and almost vestigial in the male, whereas the optic and
olfactory lobes are very large in the latter. The cortical portion

of the large worker brain is, moreover, extremely rich in cellular elements. In this connection I would request you to glance at the figures and their explanation.

Very recently, to be sure, it has come to be the fashion to underestimate the importance of brain-morphology in psychology and even in nerve-physiology. But fashions, especially such absurd ones as this, should have no influence on true investigation. Of course, we should not expect anatomy to say what it was never intended to say.

In ants, injury to the cerebrum leads to the same results as injury to the brain of the pigeon.

In this place I would refer you for a fuller account of the details of sensation and the psychic peculiarities of insects to my more extended work above mentioned: *Sensations des Insectes.*

It can be demonstrated that insects possess the senses of sight, smell, taste, and touch. The auditory sense is doubtful. Perhaps a sense of touch modified for the perception of delicate vibrations may bear a deceptive resemblance to hearing. A sixth sense has nowhere been shown to occur. A photodermatic sense, modified for light-sensation, must be regarded as a form of the tactile sense. It occurs in many insects. This sense is in no respect of an optic nature. In aquatic insects the olfactory and gustatory senses perhaps grade over into each other somewhat (Nagel), since both perceive chemical substances dissolved in the water.

The visual sense of the facetted eyes is especially adapted for seeing movements, i. e., for perceiving relative changes of position in the retinal image. In flight it is able to localise large spatial areas admirably, but must show less definite contours of the objects than our eyes. The compound eye yields only a single upright image (Exner), the clearness of which increases with the number of facets and the convexity of the eye. Exner succeeded in photographing this image in the fire-fly (Lampyris). As the eyes are immovable the sight of resting objects soon disappears so far as the resting insect is concerned. For this reason resting insects are easily captured when very slowly approached. In flight insects orient themselves in space by means of their compound

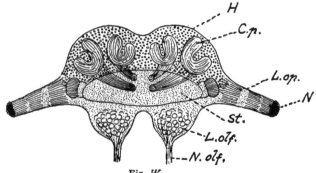

Fig. *W.*

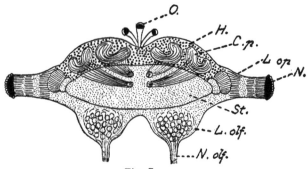

Fig. *F.*

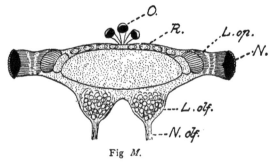

Fig *M.*

Brain (supra-œsophageal ganglion) of an ant (*Lasius fuliginosus*), magnified 60 diameters, seen from above.

Fig. *W*. Brain of the Worker.
Fig. *F*. Brain of the Queen (Female)
Fig. *M*. Brain of the Male.

St. = Brain trunk. *L. op.* = Lobus opticus (optic lobe). *L. olf.* = Lobus olfactorius sive antennalis (olfactory lobe). *N.* = Facetted eye. *N. olf.* = Nervus olfactorius sive antennalis (olfactory nerve). *O.* = Ocelli, or simple eyes with their nerves (present only in the male and queen). *H.* = Cellular brain cortex (developed only in the worker and queen). *C. p.* = Corpora pedunculata, or fungiform bodies (developed only in the worker and queen). *R.* = Rudimental cortex of male.

The length of the whole ant is :

in the worker 4.5 mm ;
in the queen 6.0 mm ;
in the male 4.5 mm.

N. B. The striation of the corpora pedunculata and their stems is represented diagrammatically, for the purpose of indicating rather coarsely their extremely delicate fibrillar structure.

eyes. Odor, when perceived, merely draws these animals in a particular direction. When the compound eyes are covered, all powers of orientation in the air are lost. Many insects can adapt their eyes for the day or night by a shifting of the pigment. Ants see the ultra-violet with their eyes. Honey-bees and humble-bees can distinguish colors, but obviously in other tones than we do, since they cannot be deceived by artificial flowers of the most skilful workmanship. This may be due to admixtures of the ultra-violet rays which are invisible to our eyes.

The ocelli (simple eyes) play a subordinate rôle, and probably serve as organs of sight for objects situated in the immediate vicinity and in dark cavities.

The olfactory sense has its seat in the antennæ, usually in the club-shaped flagellum, or rather in the pore-plates and olfactory rods of these portions of the antennæ. On account of its external and moveable position at the tip of the antenna, the olfactory organ possesses two properties which are lacking in the vertebrates, and particularly in man. These are:

1. The power of perceiving the chemical nature of a body by direct contact (contact-odor);

2. The power of space-perception and of perceiving the form of objects and that of the animal's own trail by means of odor, and the additional property of leaving associated memories.

The olfactory sense of insects, therefore, gives these animals definite and clear-cut perceptions of space-relations, and enables the animal while moving on the surface of the ground to orient itself with facility. I have designated this sense, which is thus qualitatively, i. e., in its specific energy, very different from our olfactory sense, as the topochemical (olfactory) sense. Probably the pore-plates are used for perceiving odor at a distance and the olfactory rods for contact-odor, but this is pure conjecture. Extirpation of the antennæ destroys the power of distinguishing friends from enemies and deprives the ant of the faculty of orienting itself on the ground and of finding its way, whereas it is possible to cut off three legs and an antenna without seriously impairing these powers. The topochemical sense always permits the ant to distinguish between the directions of its trail, a faculty which Bethe attributes to a mysterious polarisation. The ability to sense different odors varies enormously in different insects. An object possessing odor for one species is often odorless for other species (and for ourselves) and *vice versa.*

The gustatory organs are situated on the mouth-parts. Among insects the reactions of this sense are very similar to our own. Will accustomed some wasps to look in a particular place for honey, which he afterwards mixed with quinine. The wasps detected the substance at once, made gestures of disgust, and never returned to the honey. Mixing the honey with alum had the same result. At first they returned, but after the disagreeable gustatory experience they failed to reappear. Incidentally this is also a proof of their gustatory memory and of their powers of association.

Several organs have been found and described as auditory. But after their removal the supposed reaction to sounds persists. This would seem to indicate that a deceptive resemblance to hearing may be produced by the perception of delicate vibrations through the tactile sense (Dugès).

The tactile sense is everywhere represented by tactile hairs and papillæ. It reacts more especially to delicate tremors of the atmosphere or soil. Certain arthropods, especially the spiders, orient themselves mainly by means of this sense.

It may be demonstrated that insects, according to the species and conditions of life, use their different senses in combination for purposes of orienting themselves and for perceiving the external world. Many species lack eyes and hence also the sense of sight. In others, again, the olfactory sense is obtuse ; certain other forms lack the contact-odor sense (e. g., most Diptera).

It has been shown that the superb powers of orientation exhibited by certain aerial animals, like birds (carrier-pigeons), bees, etc., depend on vision and its memories. Movement in the air gives this sense enormous and manifold values. The semi-circular canals of the auditory organ are an apparatus of equilibrium in vertebrates and mediate sensations of acceleration and rotation (Mach-Breuer), but do not give external orientation. For the demonstration of these matters I must refer you to my work above-cited. A specific, magnetic, or other mode of orientation, independent of the known senses, does not exist.

The facts above presented constitute the basis of insect psychology. The social insects are especially favorable objects for study on account of their manifold reciprocal relationships. If in speaking of their behavior I use terms borrowed from human life, I request you, once for all, to bear in mind that these are not to be interpreted in an anthropomorphic but in an analogous sense.

THE PROVINCE OF COGNITION.

Many insects (perhaps all, in a more rudimental condition) possess memory, i. e., they are able to store up sense-impressions in their brains for subsequent use. Insects are not merely attracted directly by sensory stimuli, as Bethe imagines. Huber, myself, Fabre, Lubbock, Wasmann, Von Buttel-Reepen, have demonstrated this fact experimentally. That bees, wasps, etc., can find their way in flight through the air, notwithstanding wind and rain (and hence under circumstances precluding the existence of any possible odoriferous trail), and even after the antennæ have been cut off, to a concealed place where they have found what they desired, though this place may be quite invisible from their nest, and this even after the expiration of days and weeks, is a fact of special importance as proof of the above assertion. It can be shown that these insects recognise objects by means of their colors, their forms, and especially by their position in space. Position they perceive through the mutual relations and succession of the large objects in space, as these are revealed to them in their rapid change of place during flight in their compound eyes (shifting of retinal images). Especially the experiments performed by Von Buttel-Reepen and myself leave no doubt concerning this fact. Additional proof of a different nature is furnished by Von Buttel, who found that ether or chloroform narcosis deprives bees of all memory. By this means enemies can be converted into friends. Under these circumstances, too, all memory of locality is lost and must be reacquired by means

of a new flight of orientation.   An animal, however, certainly cannot forget without having remembered.

The topochemical antennal sense also furnishes splendid proofs
of memory in ants, bees, etc.   An ant may perform an arduous
journey of thirty meters from her ruined nest, there find a place
suitable for building another nest, return, orienting herself by
means of her antennæ, seize a companion who forthwith rolls herself about her abductrix, and is carried to the newly selected spot.
The latter then also finds her way to the original nest, and both
each carry back another companion, etc.   The memory of the suitable nature of the locality for establishing a new nest must exist in
the brain of the first ant or she would not return, laden with a companion, to this very spot.   The slave-making ants (*Polyergus*) undertake predatory expeditions, led by a few workers, who for days
and weeks previously have been searching the neighborhood for
nests of *Formica fusca*.   The ants often lose their way, remain
standing and hunt about for a long time till one or the other finds
the topochemical trail and indicates to the others the direction to
be followed by rapidly pushing ahead.   Then the pupæ of the *Formica fusca* nest, which they have found, are brought up from the
depths of the galleries, appropriated and dragged home, often a
distance of forty meters or more.   If the plundered nest still con-
tains pupæ, the robbers return on the same or following days and
carry off the remainder, but if there are no pupæ left they do not
return.   How do the Polyergus know whether there are pupæ remaining? It can be demonstrated that smell could not attract them
from such a distance, and this is even less possible for sight or any
other sense.   Memory alone, i. e., the recollection that many pupæ
still remain behind in the plundered nest can induce them to return.   I have carefully followed a great number of these predatory
expeditions.

While Formica species follow their topochemical trail with
great difficulty over new roads, they nevertheless know the immediate surroundings of their nest so well that even shovelling away
the earth can scarcely disconcert them, and they find their way at
once, as Wasmann emphatically states and as I myself have often

observed.   That this cannot be due to smelling at long range can
be demonstrated in another manner, for the olfactory powers of the
genus Formica, like those of honey-bees, are not sufficiently acute
for this purpose, as has been shown in innumerable experiments by
all connoisseurs of these animals. Certain ants can recognise friends
even after the expiration of months.   In ants and bees there are
very complex combinations and mixtures of odors, which Von Buttel has very aptly distinguished as nest-odor, colony- (family-) odor,
and individual odor.   In ants we have in addition a species-odor,
while the queen-odor does not play the same rôle as among bees.

It follows from these and many other considerations that the
social Hymenoptera can store up in their brains visual images and
topochemical odor-images and combine these to form perceptions
or something of a similar nature, and that they can associate such
perceptions, even those of different senses, especially sight, odor,
and taste, with one another and thereby acquire spatial images.

Huber as well as Von Buttel, Wasmann, and myself have
always found that these animals, through frequent repetition of an
activity, journey, etc., gain in the certainty and rapidity of the execution of their instincts.   Hence they form, very rapidly to be
sure, habits.   Von Buttel gives splendid examples of these in the
robber-bees, i. e., in some of the common honey-bees that have
acquired the habit of stealing the honey from the hives of strangers.
At first the robbers display some hesitation, though later they become more and more impudent.   But he who uses the term habit,
must imply secondary automatism and a pre-existing plastic adaptability.   Von Buttel adduces an admirable proof of this whole matter and at the same time one of the clearest and simplest refuta-
tions of Bethe's innumerable blunders, when he shows that bees
that have never flown from the hive, even though they may be
older than others that have already flown, are unable to find their
way back even from a distance of a few meters, when they are unable to see the hive, whereas old bees know the whole environment, often to a distance of six or seven kilometers.

It results, therefore, from the unanimous observations of all
the connoisseurs that sensation, perception, and association, infer-

ence, memory and habit follow in the social insects on the whole the same fundamental laws as in the vertebrates and ourselves. Furthermore, attention is surprisingly developed in insects, often taking on an obsessional character and being difficult to divert.

On the other hand, inherited automatism exhibits a colossal preponderance. The above-mentioned faculties are manifested only in an extremely feeble form beyond the confines of the in-stinct-automatism stereotyped in the species.

An insect is extraordinarily stupid and inadaptable to all things not related to its instincts. Nevertheless I succeeded in teaching a water-beetle (*Dytiscus marginalis*) which in nature feeds only in the water, to eat on my table. While thus feeding, it always exe-cuted a clumsy flexor-movement with its fore-legs which brought it over on its back. The insect learned to keep on feeding while on its back, but it would not dispense with this movement, which is adapted to feeding in the water. On the other hand, it always at-tempted to leap out of the water (no longer fleeing to the bottom of the vessel) when I entered the room, and nibbled at the tip of my finger in the most familiar manner. Now these are certainly plastic variations of instinct. In a similar manner some large Algerian ants which I transplanted to Zurich, learned during the course of the summer months to close the entrance of their nest with pellets of earth, because they were being persecuted and an-noyed by our little *Lasius niger*. In Algiers I always saw the nest-opening wide open. There are many similar examples which go to show that these tiny animals can utilise some few of their expe-riences even when this requires a departure from the usual in-stincts.

That ants, bees, and wasps are able to exchange communica-tions that are understood, and that they do not merely titillate one another with their antennæ as Bethe maintains, has been demon-strated in so many hundred instances, that it is unnecessary to waste many words on this subject. The observations of a single predatory expedition of Polyergus, with a standing still of the whole army and a seeking for the lost trail, is proof sufficient of the above statement. But, of course, this is not language in the human sense !

There are no abstract concepts corresponding to the signs. We are here concerned only with hereditary, instinctively automatic signs. The same is true of their comprehension (pushing with the head, rushing at one another with wide-open mandibles, titillation with the antennæ, stridulatory movement of the abdomen, etc.). Moreover, imitation plays a great rôle. Ants, bees, etc., imitate and follow their companions. Hence it is decidedly erroneous (and in this matter Wasmann, Von Buttel, and myself are of but one opinion) to inject human thought-conception and human ratiocination into this instinct-language, as has been done to some extent, at least, even by Pierre Huber, not to mention others. It is even very doubtful whether a so-called general sensory idea (i. e., a general idea of an object, like the idea "ant," "enemy," "nest," "pupa") can arise in the emmet brain. This is hardly capable of demonstration. Undoubtedly perception and association can be carried on in a very simple way, after the manner of insects, without ever rising to such complex results. At any rate proofs of such an assumption are lacking. But what exists is surely in itself sufficiently interesting and important. It gives us at least an insight into the brain-life of these animals.

Better than any generalisations, a good example will show what I mean.

Plateau had maintained that when Dahlia blossoms are covered with green leaves, bees nevertheless return to them at once. At first he concealed his Dahlias incompletely (i. e., only their ray-florets), afterwards completely, but still in an unsatisfactory manner, and inferred from the results that bees are attracted by odor and not by sight.

a. In a Dahlia bed visited by many bees and comprising about forty-three floral heads of different colors, I covered first seventeen and then eight at 2.15 P. M., September 10th, with grape-leaves bent around them and fastened with pins.

b. Of four I covered only the yellow disc;

c. Of one, on the other hand, I covered only the outer ray-florets, leaving the disc visible.

So many bees were visiting the Dahlias that at times there were two or three to a flower.

Result: Immediately all the completely covered flowers ceased to be visited by the bees. Dahlia (*c*) continued to be visited like those completely visible. The bees often flew to Dahlias (*b*) but at once abandoned them; a few, however, succeeded in finding the disc beneath the leaves.

Then as soon as I removed the covering from a red Dahlia the bees at once flew to it; and soon a poorly concealed specimen was detected and visited. Later an inquisitive bee discovered the entrance to a covered Dahlia from the side or from below. Thenceforth this bee, but only this one, returned to this same covered flower.

Nevertheless several bees seemed to be seeking the Dahlias which had so suddenly disappeared. Towards 5.30 o'clock some of them had detected the covered flowers. Thenceforth these insects were rapidly imitated by the other bees, and in a short time the hidden flowers were again being visited. As soon as a bee had discovered my imposition and found the entrance to a hidden flower, she flew in her subsequent journeys, without hesitation to the concealed opening of the grape-leaf. As long as a bee had merely made the discovery by herself, she remained unnoticed by the others. When this was accomplished by several, however, (usually by four or five,) the others followed their example.

Plateau, therefore, conducted his experiments in a faulty manner and obtained erroneous results. The bees still saw the Dahlias which he at first incompletely concealed. Then, by the time he had covered them up completely, but only from above, they had already detected the fraud and saw the Dahlias also from the side. Plateau had failed to take into consideration the bee's memory and attention.

September 13th I made some crude imitations of Dahlias by sticking the yellow heads of Hieracium (hawkweed) each in a Petunia flower, and placed them among the Dahlias. Neither the Petunias nor the Hieracium had been visited by the bees. Nevertheless many of the honey and humble-bees flew at first to the artefacts in almost as great numbers as to the Dahlias, but at once abandoned the flowers when they had detected the error, obviously by means of their sense of smell. The same results were produced by a Dahlia, the disc of which had been replaced by the disc of a Hieracium.

As a control experiment I had placed a beautiful, odorous Dahlia disc among the white and yellow Chrysanthemums which had been neglected by the bees. For a whole half hour the bees flew by only a few centimeters above the disc without noticing it; not till then was it visited by a bee that happened to be followed by a second. From this moment the Dahlia disc which lay in the path of flight was visited like the others, whereas on the other hand the Petunia-Hieracium artefacts, now known to be fraudulent, were no longer noticed.

Plateau has demonstrated that artificial flowers, no matter how carefully copied from the human standpoint, are not noticed by insects. I placed artefacts of this description among the Dahlias. They remained in fact entirely neglected. Perhaps, as above suggested, the bees are able to distinguish the chlorophyll colors from other artificial hues, owing to admixtures of the ultra-violet rays, or by some other means. But since Plateau imagines that the artificial flowers repel insects, I cut out, Sept. 19th, the following rather crude paper-flowers:

a. A red flower;

β. A white flower;

γ. A blue flower;

δ A blue flower, with a yellow center made from a dead leaf;

ε. A rose-colored piece of paper with a dry Dahlia disc;

ζ. A green Dahlia leaf (unchanged).

It was nine o'clock in the morning. I placed a drop of honey on each of the six artefacts mounted among the Dahlias. For a quarter of an hour many bees flew past, very close to my artefacts but without perceiving and hence without smelling the honey. I went away for an hour. On my return artefact δ was without honey, and must therefore have been discovered by the bees. All the others had remained quite untouched and unnoticed.

With some difficulty I next undertook to bring artefact *a* very close to a bee resting on a Dahlia. But the attention of the bee was so deeply engrossed by the Dahlia that I had to repeat the experiment four or five times till I succeeded in bringing the honey within reach of her proboscis. The insect at once began to suck up the honey from the paper-flower. I marked the bee's back with blue paint so that I might be able to recognise her, and repeated the experiment with *β* and *ε*. In these cases one of the bees was painted yellow, the other white.

Soon the blue bee, which had in the meantime gone to the hive, returned, flew at once to *a*, first hovering about it dubiously, then to *δ*, where she fed, then again to *a*, but not to the Dahlias. Later the yellow bee returned to *β* and fed, and flew to *a* and *δ* where she again fed, but gave as little heed to the Dahlias as did the blue bee.

Thereupon the white bee returned seeking *ε*, but failing to find it, at once went to feeding on some of the Dahlias. But she tarried only a moment on each Dahlia as if tortured by the *idée fixe* of honey. She returned to the artefacts, the perception of which, however, she was not quite able to associate with the memory of the honey flavor. At last she found a separate piece of *ε*, which happened to be turned down somewhat behind, and began lapping up the honey.

Thenceforth the three painted bees, and these alone, returned regularly to the artefacts and no longer visited the Dahlias. The fact is of great importance that the painted bees entirely of their own accord, undoubtedly through an instinctive inference from analogy, discovered the other artefacts as soon as their attention had been attracted by the honey on one of them, notwithstanding the fact that the artefacts were some distance from one another and of different colors. For were not the Dahlias, too, which they had previously visited, of different colors? Thus the blue bee flew to *a*, *β*, *γ*, and *δ*, the yellow to *β*, *a*, *δ*, and *γ*, the white *ε*, *a*, *β*, and *δ*. Matters continued thus for half an hour. The hidden green *ζ* was not found, evidently because it was indistinguishable from the green foliage.

Finally one bee, by herself, having had in all probability her attention attracted by the three others, came to δ and fed. I marked her with carmine. Thereupon she flew to α and drove the blue bee away. Another bee was attracted to ε of her own accord and was painted with cinnobar. Still another bee came by herself to β and was painted green. It was now 12.30 o'clock. The experiment had therefore lasted more than three hours, and during this time only six bees had come to know the artefacts, while the great majority still kept on visiting the Dahlias. But now the other bees began to have their attention attracted by the visitors to the artefacts. One, then two, then three, and finally more new ones followed, and I had not sufficient colors with which to mark them. Every moment I was obliged to replenish the honey. Then I went to dinner and returned at 1.25. At this moment seven bees were feeding on β, two on α, one on γ, three on δ, the white one alone on ε. More than half of all these were new, unpainted followers. Now a veritable swarm of bees threw themselves on the artefacts and licked up the last traces of the honey. Then for the first time, after more than four hours, a bee from the swarm discovered the honey on the artefact ζ, which on account of its color had remained concealed up to this time!

As a pack of hounds throws itself on an empty skeleton, the swarm of bees, now completely diverted from the Dahlias, cast themselves on the completely empty artefacts and vainly searched every corner of them for honey. It was 1.55 P. M. The bees began to scatter and return to the Dahlias. Then I replaced α and β by a red and white paper respectively, which had never come in contact with honey and could not therefore smell of the substance. These pieces of paper, nevertheless, were visited and examined by various bees, whose brains were still possessed with the fixed idea of the flavor of honey. The white bee, e. g., investigated the white paper very carefully for a period of three to four minutes. There could, of course, be no such thing as an unknown force or attraction of odor, or brilliancy of floral colors. This fact can only be explained by an association of space, form, and color memories with memories of taste.

Thereupon I took all the artefacts in my left hand for the purpose of carrying them away. Two or three bees followed me, hovering about my left hand, and tried to alight on the empty artefacts. The space-image had changed and only the color and form could any longer be of service to the bees in their recognition of these objects.

This experiment is so clear and unequivocal that I mention it here among many others. It demonstrates:

1. The space, form, and color perceptions of the honey-bee. That these are possible only through the agency of the compound eyes is proved by other experiments (varnishing the eyes, extirpation of the antennæ, mouth-parts, etc.).

2. The memory of the honey-bee, in particular her visual and gustatory memory.

3. Her power of associating gustatory with visual memories.

4. Her ability instinctively to draw inferences from analogy: If she has once been offered honey in an artefact, she will investigate others, even those of a different color and hitherto unnoticed. These she compares by means of the visual sense, since they are relatively similar, and recognises them as similar though such objects are most unusual in the bee's experience.

5. Her poor olfactory sense, which is useful only at very close range.

6. The onesidedness and narrow circle of her attention.

7. The rapid formation of habits.

8. The limits of imitation of bees by one another.

Of course, I should not allow myself to draw these conclusions from a single experiment, if they had not been confirmed by innumerable observations by the ablest investigators in this field. Lubbock showed clearly that it is necessary to train a bee for some time to go to a particular color if one wishes to compel her to pay no attention to other colors. This is the only way in which it is possible to demonstrate her ability to distinguish colors. My bees, on the contrary, had been trained on differently colored objects (Dahlias and artefacts) and therefore paid no attention to differences in color. It would be a fallacy to conclude from this that they do not distinguish colors. On the contrary, by means of other experiments I have fully confirmed Lubbock's results.

By 2.20 P. M. all of my bees, even the painted ones, had re-turned to the Dahlias.

On September 27, a week later, I wished to perform a fresh experiment with the same bees. I intended to make them distin-guish between differently colored discs, placed at different points on a long scale, representing on a great sheet of paper, varying intensi-ties of light from white through gray to black. First, I wished to train a bee to a single color. But I had calculated without the bee's memory, which rendered the whole experiment impracticable. Scarcely had I placed my paper with the discs on the lawn near the Dahlia bed, and placed one or two bees on the blue discs and marked them with colors, when they began to investigate all the red, blue, white, black and other discs with or without honey. After a few moments had elapsed, other bees came from the Dahlia bed and in a short time a whole swarm threw itself on the paper discs. Of course, those that had been provided with honey were most vis-ited, because they detained the bees, but even the discs without honey were stormed and scrutinised by bees following one another in their flight. The bees besieged even the paint-box. Among these there was one that I had previously deprived of her antennæ. She had previously partaken of the honey on the blue discs and had returned to the hive. This bee examined the blue piece of paint in the color-box.

In brief, my experiment was impossible, because all the bees still remembered from a former occasion the many-colored artefacts provided with honey, and therefore examined all the paper discs no matter of what color. The association between the taste of the honey and the paper discs had been again aroused by the sight-perception of the latter, and had acquired both consistency and rapid and powerful imitation, because honey happened to be actually found on some of the discs.

Together with the perceptive and associative powers, the power of drawing simple, instinctive inferences from analogy is also apparent. Without this, indeed, the operation of perception

and memory would be inconceivable! We have just given an example. I have shown on a former occasion that humble-bees,
whose nest I had transferred to my window, when they returned
home often confounded other windows of the same façade and examined them for a long time before they discovered the right one.
Lubbock reports similar facts. Von Buttel shows that bees that
are accustomed to rooms and windows, learn to examine the rooms
and windows in other places, i. e., other houses. When Pissot
suspended wire netting with meshes twenty-two mm. in diameter
in front of a wasp nest, the wasps hesitated at first, then went
around the netting by crawling along the ground or avoided it in
some other way. But they soon learned to fly directly through the
meshes. The sense of sight, observed during flight, is particularly
well adapted to experiments of this kind, which cannot therefore
be performed with ants. But the latter undoubtedly draw similar
inferences from the data derived from their topochemical antennal
sense. The discovery of prey or other food on a plant or an object induces these insects to examine similar plants or objects and
to perform other actions of a like nature.

There are, on the other hand, certain very stupid insects, like
the males of ants, the Diptera and may-flies (Ephemerids) with
rudimental brains, incapable of learning anything or of combining
sense-impressions to any higher degree than as simple automatisms,
and without any demonstrable retention of memory-images. Such
insects lead a life almost exclusively dominated by sensory stimuli;
but their lives are adapted to extremely simple conditions. In
these very instances the difference is most striking, and they demonstrate most clearly through comparison and contrast the *plus*
possessed by more intelligent insects.

THE REALM OF WILL.

The notion of volition, in contradistinction to the notion of
reflex action, presupposes the expiration of a certain time interval
and the operation of mediating and complex brain-activities between the sense-impression and the movement which it conditions.
In the operation of the purposeful automatisms of instinct which

arouse one another into activity in certain sequences, there is also a time interval, filled out by internal, dynamic brain-processes as in the case of the will.   Hence these are not pure reflexes.   They may for a time suffer interruption and then be again continued. But their operation is brought about in great measure by a concatenation of complicated reflexes which follow one another in a compulsory order.   On this account the term automatism or instinct is justifiable.

If we are to speak of will in the narrower sense, we must be able to establish the existence of individual decisions, which can be directed according to circumstances, i. e., are modifiable, and may, for a certain period, remain dormant in the brain to be still performed notwithstanding.   Such volition may be very different from the complex volition of man, which consists of the resultants of prodigiously manifold components that have been long preparing and combining.   The ants exhibit positive and negative volitional phenomena, which cannot be mistaken.   The ants of the genus Formica Linné are particularly brilliant in this respect, and they also illustrate the individual psychical activities most clearly.   The above-mentioned migrations from nest to nest show very beautifully the individual plans of single workers carried out with great tenacity.   For hours at a time an ant may try to overcome a multitude of difficulties for the purpose of attaining an aim which she has set herself.   This aim is not accurately prescribed by instinct, as the insect may be confronted with several possibilities, so that it often happens that two ants may be working in opposition to each other.   This looks like stupidity to the superficial observer. But it is just here that the ant's plasticity reveals itself.   For a time the two little animals interfere with each other, but finally they notice the fact, and one of them gives in, goes away, or assists the other.

These conditions are best observed during the building of nests or roads, e. g., in the horse-ant (*Formica rufa*) and still better in *F. pratensis*.   It is necessary, however, to follow the behavior of a few ants for hours, if one would have a clear conception of this matter, and for this much patience and much time are necessary.

The combats between ants, too, show certain very consistent aims of behavior, especially the struggles which I have called chronic combats (*combats à froid*). After two parties (two colonies brought together) have made peace with each other, one often sees a few individuals persecuting and maltreating certain individuals of the opposite party. They often carry their victims a long distance off, for the purpose of excluding them from the nest. If the ant that has been borne away returns to the nest and is found by her persecutrix, she is again seized and carried away to a still greater distance. In one such case in an artificial nest of a small species of Leptothorax, the persecuting ant succeeded in dragging her victim to the edge of my table. She then stretched out her head and allowed her burden to fall on the floor. This was not chance, for she repeated the performance twice in succession after I had again placed the victim on the table. Among the different individuals of the previously hostile, but now pacified opposition, she had concentrated her antipathy on this particular ant and had tried to make her return to the nest impossible. One must have very strong preconceived opinions if in such and many similar cases one would maintain that ants are lacking in individual decision and execution. Of course, all these things happen within the confines of the instinct-precincts of the species, and the different stages in the exetion of a project are instinctive. Moreover, I expressly defend myself against the imputation that I am importing human reflection and abstract concepts into this volition of the ant, though we must honestly admit, nevertheless, that in the accomplishment of our human decisions both hereditary and secondary automatisms are permitted to pass unnoticed. While I am writing these words, my eyes operate with partially hereditary, and my hand with secondary automatisms. But it goes without saying that only a human brain is capable of carrying out my complex innervations and my concomitant abstract reflections. But the ant must, nevertheless, associate and consider somewhat in a concrete way after the manner of an ant, when it pursues one of the above-mentioned aims and combines its instincts with this special object in view. While, however, the instinct of the ant can be combined for only a few slightly different purposes, by means of a small number of plastic adaptations or associations, individually interrupted in their concatenation or *vice versa*, in the thinking human being both inherited and secondary automatisms are only fragments or instruments in the service of an overwhelming, all-controlling, plastic brain-activity. It may be said incidentally that the relative independence of the spinal chord and of subordinate brain-centers in the lower animals (and even in the lower mammals) as compared with the cerebrum, may be explained in a similar manner if they are compared with the profound dependence of these organs and their functions on the massive cerebrum in man and even to some extent in the apes. The cerebrum splits up and controls its automatisms (*divide et impera*).

While success visibly heightens both the audacity and tenacity of the ant-will, it is possible to observe after repeated failure or in consequence of the sudden and unexpected attacks of powerful enemies a form of abulic dejection, which may lead to a neglect of the most important instincts, to cowardly flight, to the devouring or casting away of offspring, to neglect of work, and similar conditions. There is a chronically cumulative discouragement in degenerate ant-colonies and an acute discouragement when a combat is lost. In the latter case one may see troops of large powerful ants fleeing before a single enemy, without even attempting to defend themselves, whereas the latter a few moments previously would have been killed by a few bites from the fleeing individuals. It is remarkable how soon the victor notices and utilises this abulic discouragement. The dejected ants usually rally after the flight and soon take heart and initiative again. But they offer but feeble resistance, e. g., to a renewed attack from the same enemy on the following day. Even an ant's brain does not so soon forget the defeats which it has suffered.

In bitter conflicts between two colonies of nearly equal strength the tenacity of the struggle and with it the will to conquer increases till one of the parties is definitively overpowered. In the realm of will imitation plays a great rôle. Even among ants protervity and dejection are singularly contagious.

THE REALM OF FEELING.

It may perhaps sound ludicrous to speak of feelings in insects. But when we stop to consider how profoundly instinctive and fixed is our human life of feeling, how pronounced are the emotions in our domestic animals, and how closely interwoven with the impulses, we should expect to encounter emotions and feelings in animal psychology. And these may indeed be recognised so clearly that even Uexkuell would have to capitulate if he should come to know them more accurately. We find them already interwoven with the will as we have described it. Most of the emotions of insects are profoundly united to the instincts. Of such a nature is the jealousy of the queen bee when she kills the rival princesses, and the terror of the latter while they are still within their cells; such is the rage of fighting ants, wasps, and bees, the above-mentioned discouragement, the love of the brood, the self-devotion of the worker honey-bees, when they die of hunger while feeding their queen, and many other cases of a similar description. But there are also individual emotions that are not compelled altogether by instinct, e. g., the above-mentioned mania of certain ants for maltreating some of their antagonists. On the other hand, as I have shown, friendly services (feeding), under exceptional circumstances, may call forth feelings of sympathy and finally of partnership, even between ants of differents species. Further than this, feelings of sympathy, antipathy, and anger among ants may be intensified by repetition and by the corresponding activities, just as in other animals and man.

The social sense of duty is instinctive in ants, though they exhibit great individual, temporary, and occasional deviations, which betray a certain amount of plasticity.

PSYCHIC CORRELATIONS.

I have rapidly reviewed the three main realms of ant-psychology. It is self-evident that in this matter they no more admit of sharp demarcation from one another than elsewhere. The will consists of centrifugal resultants of sense-impressions and feelings and in turn reacts powerfully on both of these.

It is of considerable interest to observe the antagonism between different perceptions, feelings, and volitions in ants and bees, and the manner in which in these animals the intensely fixed (obsessional) attention may be finally diverted from one thing to another. Here experiment is able to teach us much. While bees are busy foraging on only one species of flower, they overlook everything else, even other flowers. If their attention is diverted by honey offered them directly, although previously overlooked, they have eyes only for the honey. An intense emotion, like the swarming of honey-bees (von Buttel) compells these insects to forget all animosities and even the old maternal hive to which they no longer return. But if the latter happens to be painted blue, and if the swarming is interrupted by taking away the queen, the bees recollect the blue color of their old hive and fly to hives that are painted blue. Two feelings often struggle with each other in bees that are "crying" and without a queen: that of animosity towards strange bees and the desire for a queen. Now if they be given a strange queen by artificial means, they kill or maltreat her, because the former feeling at first predominates. For this reason the apiarist encloses the strange queen in a wire cage. Then the foreign odor annoys the bees less because it is further away and they are unable to persecute the queen. Still they recognise the specific queen-odor and are able to feed her through the bars of the cage. This suffices to pacify the hive. Then the second feeling quickly comes to the front; the workers become rapidly inured to the new odor and after three or four days have elapsed, the queen may be liberated without peril.

It is possible in ants to make the love of sweets struggle with the sense of duty, when enemies are made to attack a colony and honey is placed before the ants streaming forth to defend their nest. I have done this with *Formica pratensis*. At first the ants partook of the honey, but only for an instant. The sense of duty conquered and all of them without exception, hurried forth to battle and most of them to death. In this case a higher decision of instinct was victorious over the lower impulse.

In *résumé* I would lay stress on the following general conclusions:

1. From the standpoint of natural science we are bound to hold fast to the psychophysiological theory of identity (Monism) in contradistinction to dualism, because it alone is in harmony with the facts and with the law of the conservation of energy.

Our mind must be studied simultaneously both directly from within and indirectly from without, through biology and the conditions of its origin. Hence there is such a thing as comparative psychology of other individuals in addition to that of self, and in like manner we are led to a psychology of animals. Inference from analogy, applied with caution, is not only permissible in this science, but obligatory.

2. The senses of insects are our own. Only the auditory sense still remains doubtful, so far as its location and interpretation are concerned. A sixth sense has not yet been shown to exist, and a special sense of direction and orientation is certainly lacking. The vestibular apparatus of vertebrates is merely an organ of equilibration and mediates internal sensations of acceleration, but gives no orientation in space outside of the body. On the other hand the visual and olfactory senses of insects present varieties in the range of their competency and in their specific energies (vision of ultra-violet, functional peculiarities of the facetted eye, topochemical antennal sense and contact-odor).

3. Reflexes, instincts, and plastic, individually adaptive, central nervous activities pass over into one another by gradations. Higher complications of these central or psychic functions correspond to a more complicated apparatus of superordinated neuron-complexes (cerebrum).

4. Without becoming antagonistic, the central nervous activity in the different groups and species of animals complicates itself in two directions: (*a*) through inheritance (natural selection, etc.) of the complex, purposeful automatisms, or instincts; (*b*) through the increasingly manifold possibilities of plastic, individually adap-

tive activities, in combination with the faculty of gradually developing secondary individual automatisms (habits).

The latter mode requires many more nerve-elements. Through hereditary predispositions (imperfect instincts) of greater or less stability, it presents transitions to the former mode.

5. In social insects the correlation of more developed psychic powers with the volume of the brain may be directly observed.

6. In these animals it is possible to demonstrate the existence of memory, associations of sensory images, perceptions, attention, habits, simple powers of inference from analogy, the utilisation of individual experiences and hence distinct, though feeble, plastic, individual deliberations or adaptations.

7. It is also possible to detect a corresponding, simpler form of volition, i. e., the carrying out of individual decisions in a more or less protracted time-sequence, through different concatenations of instincts; furthermore different kinds of discomfort and pleasure emotions, as well as interactions and antagonisms between these diverse psychic powers.

8. In insect behavior the activity of the attention is one-sided and occupies a prominent place. It narrows the scope of behavior and renders the animal temporarily blind (inattentive) to other sense-impressions.

Thus, however different may be the development of the automatic and plastic, central neurocyme activities in the brains of different animals, it is surely possible, nevertheless, to recognise certain generally valid series of phenomena and their fundamental laws.

Even to-day I am compelled to uphold the seventh thesis which I established in 1877 in my habilitation as *privat-docent* in the University of Munich:

"All the properties of the human mind may be derived from the properties of the animal mind."

I would merely add to this:

"And all the mental attributes of higher animals may be derived from those of lower animals." In other words: The doctrine of evolution is quite as valid in the province of psychology as it is in all the other provinces of organic life. Notwithstanding all the differences presented by animal organisms and the conditions of their existence, the psychic functions of the nerve-elements seem nevertheless, everywhere to be in accord with certain fundamental laws, even in the cases where this would be least expected on account of the magnitude of the differences.

APPENDIX.

THE PECULIARITIES OF THE OLFACTORY SENSE IN INSECTS.

Our sense of smell, like our sense of taste, is a chemical sense. But while the latter reacts only to substances dissolved in liquids and with but few (about five) different principal qualities, the olfactory sense reacts with innumerable qualities to particles of the most diverse substances dissolved in the atmosphere. Even to our relatively degenerate human olfactories, the number of these odor-qualities seems to be almost infinite.

In insects that live in the air and on the earth the sense of taste seems to be located, not only like our own, in the mouth-parts, but also to exhibit the same qualities and the corresponding reactions. At any rate it is easy to show that these animals are usually very fond of sweet, and dislike bitter things, and that they perceive these two properties only after having tasted of the respective substances. F. Will, in particular, has published good experiments on this subject.

In aquatic insects the conditions are more complicated. Nagel, who studied them more closely, shows how difficult it is in these cases to distinguish smell from taste, since substances dissolved in water are more or less clearly perceived or discerned from a distance by both senses and sought or avoided in consequence. Nagel, at any rate, succeeded in showing that the palpi, which are of less importance in terrestrial insects, have an important function in aquatic forms.

In this place we are concerned with an investigation of the sense of smell in terrestrial insects. Its seat has been proved to be

in the antennæ. A less important adjunct to these organs is located,
as Nagel and Wasmann have shown, in the palpi. In the antennæ
it is usually the club or foliaceous or otherwise formed dilatations
which accommodate the cellular ganglion of the antennary nerve.
I shall not discuss the histological structure of the nerve-terminations
but refer instead to Hicks, Leydig, Hauser, my own investigations and the other pertinent literature, especially to K. Kraepe-
lin's excellent work. I would merely emphasise the following
points:

1. All the olfactory papillæ of the antennæ are transformed,
hair-like pore-canals.

2. All of these present a cellular dilatation just in front of the
nerve-termination.

3. Tactile hairs are found on the antennæ together with the
olfactory papillæ.

4. The character and form of the nerve-terminations are highly
variable, but they may be reduced to three principal types: pore-
plates, olfactory rods, and olfactory hairs. The two latter are
often nearly or quite indistinguishable from each other. The nerve-
termination is always covered with a cuticula which may be never
so delicate.

Other end-organs of the Hymenopteran antenna described by
Hicks and myself, are still entirely obscure, so far as their function
is concerned, but they can have nothing to do with the sense of
smell, since they are absent in insects with a delicate sense of smell
(wasps) and accur in great numbers in the honey-bees, which have
obtuse olfactories.

That the antennæ and not the nerve-terminations of the mouth
and palate function, as organs of smell, has been demonstrated by
my control experiments, which leave absolutely no grounds for
doubt and have, moreover, been corroborated on all sides. Terrestrial insects can discern chemical substances at a distance by
means of their antennæ only. But in touch, too, these organs are
most important and the palpi only to a subordinate extent, namely
in mastication. The antennæ enable the insect to perceive the
chemical nature of bodies and in particular, to recognise and dis-

tinguish plants, other animals and food, except in so far as the visual and gustatory senses are concerned in these activities. These two senses may be readily eliminated, however, since the latter functions only during feeding and the former can be removed by varnishing the eyes or by other means. Many insects, too, are blind and find their way about exclusively by means of their antennæ. This is the case, e. g., with many predatory ants of the genus Eciton.

But I will here assume these questions to be known and answered, nor will I indulge in polemics with Bethe and his associates concerning the propriety of designating the chemical antennal sense as "smell." I have discussed this matter elsewhere.[1] What I wish to investigate in this place is the psychological quality of the antennal olfactory sense, how it results in part from observation and in part from the too little heeded correlative laws of the psychological exploitation of each sense in accordance with its structure. I assume as known the doctrines of specific energies and adequate stimuli, together with the more recent investigations on the still undifferentiated senses, like photodermatism and the like, and would refer, moreover, to Helmholtz's *Die Thatsachen in der Wahrnehmung*, 1879. Hirschwald, Berlin.

When in our own human subjective psychology, which alone is known to us directly, we investigate the manner in which we interpret our sensations, we happen upon a peculiar fact to which especially Herbert Spencer has called attention. We find that so-called perceptions consist, as is well known, of sensations which are bound together sometimes firmly, sometimes more loosely. The more intimately the sensations are bound together to form a whole, the easier it is for us to recall in our memory the whole from a part. Thus, e. g., it is easy for me to form an idea from the thought of the head of an acquaintance as to the remainder of his body. In the same manner the first note of a melody or the first verse of a poem brings back the remainder of either. But the thought of an

---

[1] "Sensations des Insectes," *Rivista di Biologia Generale.* Como, 1900–1901. For the remainder see also A. Forel, *Mitth. des Münchener entom. Vereins,* 1878, and *Recueil. Zool. Suisse,* 1886–1887.

odor of violets, a sensation of hunger, or a stomach-ache, are incapable of recalling in me either simultaneous or subsequent odors or feelings.

These latter conditions call up in my consciousness much more easily certain associated visual, tactile, or auditory images (e. g., the visual image of a violet, a table set for a meal). As ideas they are commonly to be represented in consciousness only with considerable difficulty, and sometimes not at all, and they are scarcely capable of association among themselves. We readily observe, moreover, that visual images furnish us mainly with space recollections, auditory images with sequences in time, and tactile images with both, but less perfectly. These are indubitable and well-known facts.

But when we seek for the wherefore of these phenomena, we find the answer in the structure of the particular sense-organ and in its manner of functioning.

It is well known that the eye gives us a very accurate image of the external world on our retina. Colors and forms are there depicted in the most delicate detail, and both the convergence of our two eyes and their movement and accommodation gives us besides the dimensions of depth through stereoscopic vision. Whatever may be still lacking or disturbing is supplied by instinctive inferences acquired by practice, both in memory and direct perception (like the lacunæ of the visual field), or ignored (like the turbidity of the corpus vitreum). But the basis of the visual image is given in the coördinated *tout ensemble* of the retinal stimuli, namely the retinal image.[1] Hence, since the retina furnishes us with such spatial projections, and these in sharp details, or relations, definitely coördinated with one another, the sense of sight gives us knowledge of space. For this reason, also, and solely on this account, we find it so easy to supply through memory by asso-

---

[1] It is well known that in this matter the movements of the eyes, the movements of the body and of external objects play an essential part, so that without these the eye would fail to give us any knowledge of space. But I need not discuss this further, since the antennæ of ants are at least quite as moveable and their olfactory sense is even more easily educated in unison with the tactile sense.

ciation the missing remnant of a visual spatial image. For this reason, too, the visual sensations are preëminently associative or relational in space, to use Spencer's expression. For the same reason the insane person so readily exhibits halucinations of complicated spatial images in the visual sphere. This would be impossible in the case of the olfactory sense.

Similarly, the organ of Corti in the ear gives us tone or sound scales in accurate time-sequence, and hence also associations of sequence much more perfectly than the other senses. Its associations are thus in the main associations of sequence, because the end-apparatus registers time-sequences in time-intervals and not as space images.

The corresponding cortical receptive areas are capable, in the first instance, merely of registering what is brought to them by the sense-stimuli and these are mainly associated spatial images for sight and tone or sound-sequences for hearing.

Let us consider for a moment how odors strike the mucous membranes of our choanæ. They are wafted towards us as wild mixtures in an airy maelstrom, which brings them to the olfactory terminations without order in the inhaled air or in the mucous of the palate. They come in such a way that there cannot possibly be any spatial association of the different odors in definite relationships. In time they succeed one another slowly and without order, according to the law of the stronger element in the mixture, but without any definite combination. If, after one has been inhaling the odor of violets, the atmosphere gradually becomes charged with more roast meat than violet particles, the odor of roast succeeds that of violet. But nowhere can we perceive anything like a definitely associated sequence, so that neither our ideas of time nor those of space comprise odors that revive one another through association. By much sniffing of the surface of objects we could at most finally succeed in forming a kind of spatial image, but this would be very difficult owing to man's upright posture. Nevertheless it is probable that dogs, hedge-hogs, and similar animals acquire a certain olfactory image by means of sniffing. The same conditions obtain in the sphere of taste and the visceral sensations for the same reasons. None of these senses furnish us with any sharply defined qualitative relations either in space or time. On this account they furnish by themselves no associations, no true perceptions, no memory images, but merely sensations, and these often as mixed sensations, which are vague and capable of being associated only with associative senses. The hallucinations of smell, taste, and of the splanchnic sensations, are not deceptive perceptions, since they cannot have a deceptive resemblance to objects. They are simply paræsthesias or hyperæsthesias, i. e., pathological sensations of an elementary character either without adequate stimulus or inadequate to the stimulus.

The tactile sense furnishes us with a gross perception of space and of definite relations, and may, therefore, give rise to hallucinations, or false perceptions of objects. By better training its associative powers in the blind may be intensified. The visual sensations are usually associated with tactile localisations.

Thus we see that there is a law according to which the psychology of a sense depends not only on its specific energy but also on the manner in which it is able to transmit to the brain the relations of its qualities in space and time. On this depends the knowledge we acquire concerning time and space relations through a particular sense and hence also its ability to form perceptions and associations in the brain. More or less experience is, of course, to be added or subtracted, but this is merely capable of enriching the knowledge of its possessor according to the measure of the relations of the particular sense-stimuli in space and time.

I would beg you to hold fast to what I have said and then to picture to yourselves an olfactory sense, i. e., a chemical sense effective at a distance and like our sense of smell, capable of receiving impressions from particles of the most diverse substances diffused through the atmosphere, located not in your nostrils, but on your hands. For of such a nature is the position of the olfactory sense on the antennal club of the ant.

Now imagine your olfactory hands in continual vibration, touching all objects to the right and to the left as you walk along, thereby rapidly locating the position of all odoriferous objects as you approach or recede from them, and perceiving the surfaces both simultaneously and successively as parts of objects differing in odor and position. It is clear from the very outset that such sense-organs would enable you to construct a veritable odor-chart of the path you had traversed and one of double significance:

1. A clear contact-odor chart, restricted, to be sure, to the immediate environment and giving the accurate odor-form of the objects touched (round odors, rectangular odors, elongate odors, etc.) and further hard and soft odors in combination with the tactile sensations.

2. A less definite chart which, however, has orienting value for a certain distance, and produces emanations which we may picture to ourselves like the red gas of bromine which we can actually see.

If we have demonstrated that ants perceive chemical qualities through their antennæ both from contact and from a distance, then the antennæ must give them knowledge of space, if the above formulated law is true, and concerning this there can be little doubt. This must be true even from the fact that the two antennæ simultaneously perceive different and differently odoriferous portions of space.[1]

They must therefore also transmit perceptions and topographically associated memories concerning a path thus touched and smelled. Both the trail of the ants themselves and the surrounding objects must leave in their brains a chemical (odor-) space-form with different, more or less definitely circumscribed qualities, i. e., an odor-image of immediate space, and this must render associated memories possible. Thus an ant must perceive the forms of its trail by means of smell. This is impossible, at least for the majority of the species, by means of the eyes. If this is true, an ant will always be able, no matter where she may be placed on her

---

[1] It is not without interest to compare these facts with Condillac's discussion (*Treatise on the Sensations*) concerning his hypothetical statue. Condillac shows that our sense of smell is of itself incapable of giving us space knowledge. But it is different in the case of the topochemical sense of smell in combination with the antennary movements. Here Condillac's conditions of the gustatory sense are fulfilled.

trail, to perceive what is to the right, left, behind or before her,
and consequently what direction she is to take, according to whether
she is bound for home, or in the opposite direction to a tree in-
fested with Aphides, or the like.

Singularly enough, I had established this latter fact in my
"Études Myrmécologiques en 1886" (*Annales de la Société Ento-
mologique de Belgique*) before I had arrived at its theoretical interpretation. But I was at once led by this discovery in the same
work to the interpretation just given. Without knowing of my
work in this connection, A. Bethe has recently established (discovered, as he supposes) this same fact, and has designated it as
"polarisation of the ant-trail." He regards this as the expression
of a mysterious, inexplicable force, or polarisation. As we have
seen, the matter is not only no enigma, but on the contrary, a necessary psychological postulate. We should rather find the absence
of this faculty incomprehensible.

But everything I have just said presupposes a receptive brain.
The formation of lasting perceptions and associations cannot take
place without an organ capable of fixing the sense-impressions and
of combining them among themselves. Experience shows that the
immediate sensory centers are inadequate to the performance of
this task. Though undoubtedly receptive, they are, nevertheless,
incapable of utilising what has been received in the development
of more complex instincts and can turn it to account only in the
grosser, simpler reflexes and automatisms. To be sure, a male
ant has better eyes than a worker ant, and probably quite as good
antennæ, but he is unable to remember what he has seen and is
especially incapable of associating it in the form of a trail-image,
because he is almost devoid of a brain. For this reason he is unable to find his way back to the nest. On the other hand, it is well
known that the brain of a man who has lost a limb or whose hearing is defective, will enable him to paint pictures with his foot,
write with the stump of an arm or construct grand combinations
from the images of defective senses.

I venture, therefore, to designate as topochemical the olfactory
antennal sense of honey-bees, humble-bees, wasps, etc.

Can we generalise to such an extent as to apply this term without further investigation to all arthropods? To a considerable extent this must be denied.

In fact, the multiformity in the structure and development of the arthropod sense-organs is enormous, and we must exercise caution in making premature generalisations.

It is certain that in some aerial insects the olfactory sense has dwindled to a minimum, e. g., in those species in which the male recognises and follows the female exclusively by means of the eyes, as in the Odonata (dragon-flies). To insects with such habits an olfactory sense would be almost superfluous. Here, too, the antennæ have dwindled to diminutive dimensions.

But there are insects whose antennæ are immovable and quite unable to touch objects. This is the case in most Diptera (flies). Still these antennæ are often highly developed and present striking dilatations densely beset with olfactory papillæ. By experiment I have demonstrated the existence of an olfactory sense in such Dipteran antennæ, and I have been able to show that, e. g., in *Sarcophaga vivipara* and other carrion flies, the egg-laying instinct is absolutely dependent on the sensation of the odor of carrion and the presence of the antennæ. In these cases the contact-odor sense is undoubtedly absent. More or less of a topochemical odor-sense at long range must, of course, be present, since the antennæ are external, but the precision of the spatial image must be very imperfect, owing to the immobility of the antennæ. Nevertheless, flies move about so rapidly in the air that they must be able by means of their antennæ to distinguish very quickly the direction from which odors are being wafted. These insects do, in fact, find the concealed source of odors with great assurance. But this is no great art, for even we ourselves are able to do the same by sniffing or going to and fro. But the flies find their way through the air with their eyes and not at all by means of their sense of smell. Hence their olfactory powers probably constitute a closer psychological approximation to those of mammals than to the topochemical odor-sense of ants, for they can hardly furnish any constant and definite space-relations.

Even in many insects with movable antennæ and of less ærial habits, e. g., the chafers and bombycid moths, the antennal olfactory sense is evidently much better adapted to function at a distance, i. e., to the perception of odors from distant objects, than to the perception of space and trails. Such insects find their way by means of their eyes, but fly in the direction whence their antennæ perceive an odor that is being sought.

A genuine topochemical antennal sense is, therefore, probably best developed in all arthropods, whose antennæ are not only movable in the atmosphere, but adapted to feeling of objects. In these cases the still imperfect topochemical oder-sense for distances can be momentarily controlled by the contact-odor-sense and definitively fixed topographically, i. e., topochemically, as we see so extensively practised in the ants.

It would be possible to meet this view with the objection that a contact-odor sense could not accomplish much more than the tactile sense. I have made this objection to myself. But in the first place it is necessary to reckon with the facts. Now it is a fact that insects in touching objects with their antennæ mainly perceive and distinguish the chemical constitution of the objects touched and heed these very much more than they do the mechanical impacts also perceived at the same time. Secondly, the tactile sense gives only resistance and through this, form. On the other hand, the multiplicity of odors is enormòus, and it is possible to demonstrate, as I have done for the ants, and Von Buttel-Reepen for the bees, that these animals in distinguishing their different nest-mates and their enemies, betray nothing beyond the perception of extremely delicate and numerous gradations in the qualities of odors.

In combination with topochemical space-perception, these numerous odor-qualities must constitute a spatial sense which is vastly superior to the tactile sense. The whole biology of the social Hymenoptera furnishes the objective proof of this assertion.

It would certainly be well worth while to investigate this matter in other groups of arthropods which possess complex instincts.

In conclusion I will cite an example, which I have myself observed, for the purpose of illustrating the capacity of the topo-chemical olfactory sense.

The American genus Eciton comprises predatory ants that build temporary nests from which they undertake expeditions for the purpose of preying on all kinds of insects. The Ecitons follow one another in files, like geese, and are very quick to detect new hunting grounds. As "ants of visitation," like the Africo-Indian species of Dorylus, they often take possession of human dwellings, ferret about in all the crevices of the walls and rooms for spiders, roaches, mice, and even rats, attack and tear to pieces all such vermin in the course of a few hours and then carry the booty home. They can convert a mouse into a clean skeleton. They also attack other ants and plunder their nests.

Now all the workers of the African species of Dorylus and of many of the species of Eciton are totally blind, so that they must orient themselves exclusively by means of their antennal sense.

In 1899 at Faisons, North Carolina, I was fortunate enough to find a temporary nest of the totally blind little *Eciton carolinense* in a rotten log. I placed the ants in a bag and made them the sub-ject of some observations. The Eciton workers carry their elon-gate larvæ in their jaws and extending back between their legs in such a position that the antennæ have full play in front.

Their ability to follow one another and to find their way about rapidly and unanimously in new territory without a single ant go-ing astray, is incredible. I threw a handful of Ecitons with their young into a strange garden in Washington, i. e., after a long rail-way journey and far away from their nest. Without losing a mo-ment's time, the little animals began to form in files which were fully organised in five minutes. Tapping the ground continually with their antennæ, they took up their larvæ and moved away in order, reconnoitering the territory in all directions. Not a pebble, not a crevice, not a plant was left unnoticed or overlooked. The place best suited for concealing their young was very soon found, whereas most of our European ants under such conditions, i. e., in a completely unknown locality, would probably have consumed at least an hour in accomplishing the same result. The order and dispatch with which such a procession is formed in the midst of a totally strange locality is almost fabulous. I repeated the experiment in two localities, both times with the same result. The antennæ of the Ecitons are highly developed, and it is obvious that their brain is instinctively adapted to such rapid orientation in strange places.

In Colombia, to be sure, I had had opportunities of observing, not the temporary nests, but the predatory expeditions of larger Ecitons (*E. Burchelli* and *hamatum*) possessing eyes. But these in no respect surpassed the completely blind *E. carolinense* in their power of orientation and of keeping together in files. As soon as an ant perceives that she is not being followed, she turns back and follows the others. But the marvellous fact is the certainty of this recognition, the quickness and readiness with which the animals recognise their topochemical trail without hesitation. There is none of the groping about and wandering to and fro exhibited by most of our ants. Our species of Tapinoma and Polyergus alone exhibit a similar but less perfect condition. It is especially interesting, however, to watch the *perpetuum mobile* of the antennæ of the Ecitons, the lively manner in which these are kept titillating the earth, all objects, and their companions.

All this could never be accomplished by a tactile sense alone. Nor could it be brought about by an olfactory sense which furnished no spatial associations. As soon as an Eciton is deprived of its two antennæ it is utterly lost, like any other ant under the same circumstances. It is absolutely unable to orient itself further or to recognise its companions.

In combination with the powerful development of the cerebrum (*corpora pedunculata*) the topochemical olfactory sense of the antennæ constitutes the key to ant psychology. Feeling obliged to treat of the latter in the preceeding lecture, I found it necessary here to discuss in detail this particular matter which is so often misunderstood.

[In his latest *Souvenirs entomologiques* (Seventh Series) J. H. Fabre has recorded a number of ingenious experiments showing the ability of the males of Saturnia and Bombyx to find their females at great distances and in concealment.

He tried in vain (which was to have been foreseen) to conceal the female by odors which are strong even to our olfactories. The males came notwithstanding. He established the following facts : (1) Even an adverse wind does not prevent the males from finding their way ; (2) if the box containing the female is loosely closed, the males come nevertheless ; (3) if it is hermetically closed (e. g., with wadding or soldered) they no longer come ; (4) the female must have settled for some time on a particular spot before the males come ; (5) if the female is then suddenly placed under a wire netting or a bell-jar, though still clearly visible, *the males neverthe-less do not fly to her, but pass on to the spot where she had previously rested and left her odor* ; (6) the experiment of cutting off the antennæ proves very little. The males without antennæ do not, of course, come again ; but even the other males usually come only once : their lives are too short and too soon exhausted.

At first Fabre did not wish to believe in smell, but he was compelled finally, as a result of his own experiments, to eliminate sight and hearing. Now he makes a bold hypothesis : the olfactory sense of insects has two energies, one (ours), which reacts to dissolved chemical particles, and another which receives "physical odor-waves," similar to the waves of light and sound. He already foresees how science will provide us with a "radiography of odors" (after the pattern of the Roentgen rays). But his own results, enumerated above under (4) and (5) contra-dict this view. The great distances from which the Bombyx males can discern their females is a proof to him that this cannot be due to dissolved chemical par-ticles. And these same animals smell the female only after a certain time and smell the spot where she had rested, instead of the female when she is taken away! This, however, would be inconceivable on the theory of a physical wave-sense, while it agrees very well with that of an extremely delicate, chemical olfactory sense.

It is a fact that insects very frequently fail to notice odors which we perceive as intense, and even while these are present, detect odors which are imperceptible to our olfactories. We must explain this as due to the fact that the olfactory pa-pillæ of different species of animals are especially adapted to perceiving very differ-ent substances. All biological observations favor this view, and our psycho-chem-ical theories will have to make due allowance for the fact.]

Milton Keynes UK
Ingram Content Group UK Ltd.
UKHW021104311023
431613UK00001B/5

Positive Self-Tall

SPEAK TO YOURSELF NICELY

Kindness Starts From You

BRITNEY WALSH

Table of Contents

Chapter 1:

4 Tips For Mindful Self-Compassion

Self-compassion is often a radically new way to relate to yourself. Research shows that the more you practice kindness and self-compassion through informal practices like taking a break or through formal meditation like a gentle breathing, the more self-compassion habits you develop.

Here are some tips for practicing important self-compassion that beginners and experienced meditators should remember. Self-compassion is not about kind feelings; and it's about goodwill. In other words, while a friendly and supportive attitude of self-compassion aims to alleviate suffering, we do not always have control over the situation.

The situation will only get worse if we use the practice of self-compassion to suppress or fight off suffering. With self-compassion, we consciously accept painful moments, and in return, we receive ourselves with kindness and concern, remembering that imperfections are part of the overall human experience. It gives us the support and comfort we need to cope with suffering while providing optimal conditions for growth and change and keeps us in love and connected.

1. Self-Kindness

Self-kindness is showing kindness and understanding to ourselves when we fail or suffer. Instead of criticizing or judging ourselves harshly when we are already suffering, we can acknowledge the adverse effects of our self-esteem and instead treat ourselves with warmth and patience—in short, being kind means treating our values unconditionally, even if we fall short of our expectations, whether because of our actions or even our thoughts.

2. Common Humanity

"Being part of the larger" is a prevalent concept in the positive psychology literature, and it has long been argued that the need to connect is part of human nature. Common humanity means viewing our personal experiences as inherent in the broader human experience, not as isolated or separate from others. In part, this accepts and forgives our shortcomings. Although we are imperfect, we show compassion for ourselves when we forgive ourselves for our limitations. Another aspect of humanity, in general, is not only that we are flawed or offended; Instead of isolating or isolating ourselves, we acknowledge that others sometimes feel the same way.

3. Mindfulness

In self-compassion theory, mindfulness is viewed as the opposite of avoidance or over-identification. This involves recognizing and labelling your thoughts rather than reacting to them. We become aware of our painful thoughts and feelings without diminishing their importance through reflection when we have compassion. Instead, we strike a positive balance between excessive identification on the one hand and complete avoidance of painful emotions and worries on the other.

4. Treat Yourself as You'd Treat a Friend

A good starting point is to think about how you treat others you love. So while we cannot permanently alleviate the suffering of others, we can acknowledge the existence of hell and provide support to help them overcome and grow. On this occasion:

Allow yourself to be wrong. Self-kindness and humanity come together as two separate but interconnected ideas. "We are human. But) as well as everyone else. and b) everything is normal." Instead of interpreting our thoughts, feelings, and actions as they are, we can relax when we can do the same to others. If your friend is lazy and doesn't answer the phone, you won't know right away if that friend is the wrong person. Sometimes allowing yourself to be human is one way to acknowledge your flaws and remind yourself that you are not the only imperfect person. Take care of yourself as you treat others. Closely related to the previous tip, what you understand and empathize with. If your friend is depressed, hurt, or upset, you can physically pat him on the back or hold his hand. Neff describes this as a way to connect it to our own "care system." Releases oxytocin, which has beneficial effects on the cardiovascular system.

Coupled with soft, modest words (using expressions of affection such as "Baby" or "Honey"), these gestures can make you feel proud, even if you initially resist. Of course, please don't overdo it with cute words unless it looks too weird!

Self-compassion is fundamentally refreshing. It takes a conscious effort to become aware of mental processes initially, but most worthwhile things require practice. We've looked at several different techniques for showing self-compassion regularly, so if writing a letter isn't for you, hopefully, an affirmation or a journal will help.

Chapter 2:

Five Ways Of Exuding Self-Confidence

The Master Key

Of all the keys of life, self-confidence is the master key. It is the determinant of your success in all that you do. Let's trace our steps a little bit back, what really is self-confidence? It is the ability to be bold about anything. A self-confident person can share their thoughts freely without inferiority syndrome.

The advent of technology has made this trait disappear in people. They hide behind keyboards to type their message across leaving no room for interpersonal interaction. One thing about self-confidence is that it is visible even in what you write through technology. It speaks a lot as to the kind of person you are.

Everybody has their story on how they overcame timidity. What is common in everyone is that they practice self-confidence daily, actively or passively. Some people are naturally confident while others have acquired it through practice over some time. Does it matter anyway?

Here is how you can exude self-confidence:

1. Maintain Eye Contact

Eye contact is very important when you are talking to someone either physically or via video call. Look at them in the eye anytime you are talking. This is an indication of a confident and straight person who has nothing to hide.

You can easily notice lies in the eyes of a liar. The pupils dilate when one is lying. This is an automated body response. Self-confident people have nothing to lie about.

Understandably, some people are shy. You can look at the face of the person you are talking to instead of looking away altogether. With time, you will be courageous to maintain eye contact.

2. Speak Boldly

Speaking boldly is speaking audible enough. Do not shout or whisper. Speak at the right pitch that the other person can hear. People whisper if they have something to hide. They whisper because they are unsure of what they are saying.

A confident person can repeat what they said anytime. They speak verifiable facts. Speech is a very important aspect of measuring the confidence of a person. Believe in what you are saying. Do not speak for the sake of continuing a conversation.

Self-confident people have very strong opinions about various subjects. They believe in what they stand for and are fearless. They have a coherent speech because what they say is well thought of before they speak it.

Boldness is not arrogance. Self-confident people are humble, yet they maintain bold stands on many issues.

3. A Firm Handshake

Firm greetings are a sign of self-confidence. Do not squeeze their hand or shake it loosely. Find a balance between the two.

A firm handshake is a sign of someone being sure about what they are doing. A salesperson who greets potential clients 'weakly' will not earn their trust. They appear unsure even of the products they are marketing. They have to be firm yet friendly as they interact with the market.

Greetings are mostly the first point of interaction with people. The first impression you make counts as there is never a second time to make a first impression. Self-confidence in your salutations will unlock many potential doors of opportunity.

4. Walk With Sure Steps

A confident person is known from how they walk. There are only two categories of people – Kings and slaves. Kings walk with sure steps; after all, they rule the whole kingdom. They have the authority to be anywhere at any time and nobody can question them.

On the other hand, slaves measure their steps. They walk in fear not wanting to upset their masters. They do not have that freedom.

Traditionally, blind people could know someone coming their way by listening to their steps. Sure steps signaled a confident person, mostly an authority figure.

5. Do Not Fidget

Fidgeting is a sign of weakness. Be composed whenever you are in public presence. Your non-verbal cues send many signals that can easily be read from afar. Self-confident people are calm, in public or private. They trust in their ability to overcome anything their way rather than what could be against them.

These five ways of exuding confidence are very basic. Once you master self-confidence, the sky is the limit.

Chapter 3:

Why Self-Reflection Is So Important

Practicing self-reflection in today's world is not always easy. Taking time away from your hectic schedule is nevertheless a lost art. But even so, this shouldn't always be the situation. Studies link self-reflection to personal growth, positivity, and happiness. It enables you to examine your thoughts, feelings, and actions objectively, enabling you to explore your interests and curiosities. How do you indulge yourself in self-reflection? It is about positively questioning how you think, feel, and act, what you do and why you do it, and then looking into different, better, or more efficient ways of doing it.

Here's a deeper dive into the beauty that can be found in a meaningful practice of self-reflection.

What Exactly Is Self-Reflection?

Self-reflection is a cognitive process that allows you to understand yourself better. It is the process of delving deeply into your thoughts, feelings, emotions, behaviors, desires, and motivations to discover the meaning behind "Why." It helps you gain perspective in your life.

Self-reflection allows you to gain a more in-depth understanding of your personal or professional experiences and investigate the "why" behind those experiences. That is, by asking why something happened, what impact it had, and whether or not change should occur. You are pressing into every perspective of the experience, clarifying your thinking, and zeroing in on what is truly important to you.

How Can You Practice self-reflection?

1. Identify the Key Questions

A list of pre-planned questions is an excellent way to prompt self-reflection. To better understand yourself, you must take the time to answer these questions thoughtfully. Then integrate it into a routine; you can do it daily, weekly, or monthly, whatever works best!

2. Differentiate Between Positive and Negative Reflection

Self-reflection is positive and beneficial; sometimes, reflection can turn into negative or ruminating thoughts. Reflective thoughts are intriguing, but they are either neutral or factual. Ruminating thoughts, contrarily, are more negative, judgmental, and emotionally charged.

3. Journal

Journaling can be handwritten, printed, or even an online diary app. This is an excellent way of expressing your feelings and thoughts. It allows you to look back into patterns of change and self-discovery.

4. Make Time for Self-Reflection

Self-reflection takes practice and dedication. Therefore, setting time aside allows you to hold yourself accountable for practicing it. Studies suggest starting with 10 minutes, as you step to more.

Why Is Self-Reflection Important?

1. It Gives You a Different Point of View

Emotions, in most cases, cause you to form a faulty judgment on an issue, causing you to lose focus on what matters. When you practice self-reflection in such situations, you can take a step back, process, and gain clarity. As a result, you are able to make informed decisions relevant to your needs and interests.

2. It Enables You To Respond Effectively

In most cases, we are usually quick to respond to whatever circumstances as they appear. In that reactive state, you fail to take time to process what to do or say next. As a result, you do or say something that you regret later. Self-reflection means considering the best, most productive, and beneficial course of action in a heated situation. Simply put, it allows you to think first before acting or altering any words.

3. It Enhances Learning and More Understanding

When you pause and reflect, you gain a better understanding about life. In addition to learning valuable lessons, you are able to understand what happened and why it happened the way it did. Furthermore, self-reflection allows you to evaluate and process what you've gone through. Consequently, you can then learn how to take an integrated, holistic, and healthy approach to life.

4. Enhances Your Understanding of Yourself and Others

Self-reflection allows you to understand yourself and feasibly others better. It helps you discover who you truly are. And eventually, enables you to easily find yourself, advance your purpose, be more authentic, and, most importantly, live well with others.

Conclusion

Self-reflection requires dedication and intentionality. It necessitates pausing the chaos of life and taking time to reflect and contemplate your life. When you self-reflect, you become more aware of what interests you and causes you to make changes that render growth and make your life better.

Chapter 4:

How To Gain Proper

Self-Awareness

Self-awareness is necessary across all aspects of life. In fact, those with a high level of self-awareness are happier, healthier, wealthier, and much more pleasurable than those who have a low level. You tend to thrive in relationships, decision-making, productivity, and moods if you're more self-aware. Nothing can be achieved without self-awareness!

Self-awareness is a consistent strategy that requires that you focus on different ways for personal development. It creates an opportunity to make changes in your behavior and beliefs. Remember, whatever you perceive yourself to be when you look into your mirror, is what you'll ever be.

What Is Self-Awareness?

It is the ability to see yourself clearly, understand who you are, how others perceive you, and how you fit into the world. Self-awareness is best viewed through the lens of personal growth or self-improvement.

It necessitates a greater focus on who you are and how your strengths, weaknesses, and habits inform your inner expectations. Focusing on your inner standards allows for self-improvement and, as a result, emotional intelligence.

How To Become More Self-Aware?

To become more self-aware, you'll have to adopt a scientist mind-set. Practice on yourself the same way a scientist makes prepositions and tests them to expand their knowledge and understanding. Observe how you feel, think, respond, or react to specific situations.

A high sense of self-awareness enhances your power to direct your life. You're better able to direct your thoughts and emotions, allowing you to make more intentional decisions and actions. Getting to know your authentic self is just like writing your script instead of reading someone else's. So how do you become more self-aware?

1. Understand Your Nature

To be self-aware, you must be inquisitive about yourself or who you indeed are. Your mind and body are a territory that requires action plans. Every person perceives which paths they will not partake, and ones they believe are worth trying. How far you'll go in your quest to understand yourself is determined by what you're willing to explore and experience.

2.   Look at Yourself Objectively

When you look at yourself objectively, you see yourself as you truly are. Trying to see your true personality can be a complicated process but getting to know your authentic self can be highly gratifying if you put forth the necessary effort. Once you're able to see yourself objectively, you are able to accept who you are as you work on improving yourself.

3.   Stop Being Defensive

The truth is that most people become defensive when they discover something they don't like about themselves. This makes self-awareness extremely difficult. You become self-aware when you are willing to let go of defensiveness and are open to seeing yourself in different ways from what you have always presumed. This frequently entails seeing yourself in a relatively less positive way.

4.   Ask Other's Opinions About You

Knowing how other people perceive you extend beyond face-to-face social interactions. Use that time to find out how your friends or coworkers perceive you. Be brave enough to ask them about their perceptions of you in different situations. Getting a different perspective on how you act or appear in certain situations can help you see something previously invisible to you.

5.   Keep a Journal

Journaling is indeed a great way to get started on the path to becoming more mindful. As you journal, pay close attention to how your day begins and ends. Consider what triggers may have surfaced the negative thoughts if your day was stuffed with them. Consider also what made you happy if your day was a good one.

6.   Keep Checking In

The most effective way to assess and develop self-awareness is to pause from time to time and check-in with yourself. That is, assessing your current feelings and the source of those feelings. It may appear simple, but it can be pretty challenging in practice. You'll need to bring with you a list of emotions to start this exercise.

Conclusion

Gaining insight about yourself allows you to initiate changes in your behavior and beliefs. Therefore, enabling you to change how you interpret and react to situations. Subsequently, realizing overall success will be a piece of cake because your emotional intelligence will be charged by then.

Chapter 5:

Overcoming Fear and Self-Doubt

The lack of belief most people have is the reason for their failure at even the smallest things in life. The biggest killer of dreams is the lack of belief in ourselves and the doubt of failure.

We all make mistakes. We all have some ghosts of the past that haunt us. We all have something to hide. We all have something that we regret. But what you are today is not the result of your mistakes.

You are here because of your struggles to make those things go away. You are here now with the power and strength to shape your present and your future.

Our mind is designed to take the shape of what we hold long enough inside it. The things we frequently think about ultimately start filling in the spaces within our memory, so we have to be careful. We have to decide whether we want to stay happy or to hold on to the fear we once wanted to get rid of.

The human spirit and human soul are colored by the impressions we ourselves decide to impose.

The reason why we don't want to explore the possibility of what to do is that subconsciously we don't believe that it can happen for us. We don't believe that we deserve it or if it was meant for us.

So here is something I suggest. Ask yourself, how much time in a day do you spend thinking about your dream? How much time do you spend working on your dreams everyday? What books did you read this year? What new skills have you acquired recently? What have you done that makes you worthy of your dream? Nothing?

Then you are on point with your doubt because you don't have anything to show for when the opportunity presents itself.

You don't succeed because you have this latent fear. Fear that makes you think about the consequences of what will happen if you fail even with all the good things on your hand?

I know that feeling but failure is there to teach you one important and maybe the most essential skill life can teach us; Resilience.

You rediscover your life once you have the strength to fight your every fear and every doubt because you have better things on your hand to care for.

You have another dream to pursue. Another horizon awaits you. Another peak to summit. It doesn't matter if you literally have to run to stand still. You got to do what you got to do, no matter the consequences and the sacrifices.

But failing to do what is required of you has no justifiable defense. Not even fear. Because your fears are self-imposed, and you already have many wrong things going on for you right now.

Don't let fear be one of them. Because fear is the most subtle and destructive disease So inhale all your positive energies and exhale all your doubts because you certainly are a better person without them.

Chapter 6:

Keep Moving When Things Get Hard

Keep to your goals by putting problems into perspective.

In times of difficulty, most give up.

Don't be like those people.

Difficulties are there to challenge us.

Difficulties are there to help us think outside the box.

Seek to change as you seek success.

Things never really stay the same.

Paths are never that straight.

You always come to a fork in the road.

Think of this new life and realise that thoughts will change how you act.

To have of a better life you must first consider losing this one you have now.

To achieve an extreme desired change you lose everything in the process.

It can be a tough pill to swallow.

It can be hard to see the silver lining.

But if you can keep moving towards what you have in mind,

sooner or later the new life will start to take shape.

First you must be unwavering in your faith.

It will get hard before it gets easy.

You must endure the winter to see the spring and summer.

You must weather the storm to see the sunshine.

Hard times come to all those who seek success.

Your courage will be tested.

Your endurance and persistence will be tested.

No one is exempt from this price.

You will find that nearly all your life's problems come from fear, loss, and pain,

but they are not as powerful as they appear.

They are no match for you if you believe that.

They are illusions.

Illusions because they are only real in our minds if we allow them to fester.

Most of your perceived problems never actually happened.

Most of your fears were phantoms of the mind.

Be prepared to lose it all if you desire a new life.

You must push through the pain to receive the gain.

In times of pain and struggle, you will grow.

In times of uncertainty, your bravery will shine through.

If you persist, you will make it through any problem.

You will become successful.

You must defeat the 3 phantoms to reach the promised land of health, happiness and wealth.

Self-mastery is not a battle with yourself.

Self-mastery is letting your inner-self take control.

The more you listen to your gut feeling the better your choices.

Your inner voice knows far more than your brain can tell you.

Problems arise because you have not taken action.

Force that change upon yourself.

You are like a shark.

You will die if you stop moving forward.

You will die if you accept defeat.

You must move forward like a shark.

No matter what,

Just keep swimming.

No matter what,

Get to your desired location

Get tough with yourself.

The outcome hangs in the balance.

Trust your inner compass to guide you.

Help who you can along the way.

Your thoughts will become reality good or bad.

Remain focus on the good despite the bad.

Lasting success is waiting for you.

YOU WILL MAKE IT as long as YOU DON'T QUIT!

Persistence is key.

Persist in getting what you want.

Persist in fighting for the job you desire.

Never give up even if you get rejected 100 times over.

Persistence always pays off.

You will be given your chance to shine if you keep at it.

Life will throw you curveballs.

As long as you are moving forward, you can still change direction.

Keep the dream in mind as you navigate through this uncharted territory.

No matter what,

Belief in yourself and your vision.

Keep trying to find the best people for your organization and look after them like family.

One action can change your whole situation.

One action can change your entire life.

You will overcome the obstacles if you keep going and keep believing.

Nothing is more powerful than a made-up mind.

Chapter 7:

Never Give Up – 3 Reasons to Carry on Believing in Yourself During Dark Times

We all have black moments. Sometimes these stretch into days, weeks and even months. Both small and huge problems can quickly overwhelm us. There are many reasons.

When we are really down, it may begin to feel like we are living a lifetime of hell. We get caught up in a swirling torrent of negativity. Light and hope fade. Emotionally and psychologically, we become spent. At the extreme, we might even begin to tell ourselves that we will never achieve success, happiness and joy ever again.

Avoiding sinking deeper and deeper into an unpleasant pit of despair can be avoided!

You need to recognize tipping points quickly. It is our cue to stop! Before you go down this rabbit hole, get proper perspective. The sooner the better. Think about it:

1. Stop Focusing Predominantly on Others

Do you still primarily look for external validation? Constantly worrying. For example, what your father wanted you to become? What he thinks of you because you flunked out of university? What he is going to say now when he hears your boss said you are the worst sales performer this month! His views on you facing the horrible prospect of unemployment.

Everyone sees things differently. Actually, accepting we have very little control of what others think, feel and do is helpful. Making paramount what we think, feel and do about our life's direction and quality makes all the different. By doing this we no longer need anyone else's stamp of approval.

When we stop seeking others validation, we start seeking an authentic life. It suddenly becomes uniquely ours. Self-endorsement also feels good. Giving ourselves permission to take charge and chart our own course offers a sense of freedom. We begin to see clearly that at the end of the day, we are the best judges of our lives. It can become well lived on our terms. Let go of the rest.

2. Stop Believing Things Will Not Change

Past regrets aside, recognize you are in the here and now. Without that university degree you are never going to be that doctor your father wanted! However, you do have new options every moment. Seeing new and even creative opportunities during difficulties is the ultimate determinant of your ability to bounce back, turn things around and pursue a brighter future. Short of being fired or dying, there is still time to become the top sales person. It depends if you want it enough.

Think about the different periods, people and situations in your life. Each of us is living proof of constant change. We certainly can't stop the cycle of change. Our only option is really how we respond to the constant flow. Growth and progress are about making the most of change including obstacles and challenges. Often, we will deny the inevitability of change in an attempt to try avoid confronting our worst fears. We may fail. Again, and yet again. We need to find the courage to go for it irrespective. Committing to the idea that embracing change gives us another opportunity to get better and learn. Current results are temporary and stepping stones.

3. Stop Not Seeing Your Worth

When important people in our lives tell us that we are not good enough, it can be earth shattering. When we tell ourselves, we are not good enough, this is outright dangerous. Especially so if we are astute enough to know that the most significant opinion in our life is our own. Any lack of self-worth limits potential to come out undamaged from dark periods. We can get over the bosses' views that we will never cut it as a high-flying sales guru. But it becomes impossible to lift ourselves up and see the light when we forget our own brilliance and essence. We must self-affirm to create self-love. We need to know our worth even when others miss it.

It is a crucial part of life's journey to find one's true self. This can mean deciding to change a sales career at any point, including to that of a life as a nomad. We need to make choices that maximize our sense of self-worth, not erode it. There is no prescribe perfect life trajectory. Once we can measure ourselves as much for our internal achievements, as by our external achievements in the world, we would have found hidden treasure. Self-worth is the cornerstone of mental health and stability. Block by block we can build this foundation as a fortress against any and all negative onslaughts that come our way.

So, if we remain focused on these 3 important thoughts, we will strengthen our innate ability to survive whatever life throws our way. Resilience becomes our armor as we conquer our demons. Whatever shape or size they may appear in. We are ready.

Chapter 8:

How To Accept Yourself No Matter What

There are many reasons why it may be difficult to accept yourself. Just hearing one that resonates for you can bring relief because you realize you are not alone — someone else has been there, someone else understands.

Here are some of the reasons self-acceptance can be hard and the antidotes you can practice to gradually accept yourself more and more—step one and two from the change steps listed above.

See which ones resonate for you.

1. You Think You're at Fault

You may blame yourself for something that happened in your life, especially events that may have occurred in your early years. For example, you may believe you're the cause of conflict in your parents' relationship or even their divorce.

Antidote: Give the responsibility back. It was never yours to own.

2. You Think You're Not Worthy

You began to feel inadequate as a child and carried that belief into your adult life.

Antidote: You are worthy simply because you exist. In between your confusion, self-doubt, and angst, there is so much goodness in you. Instead of focusing on your failings, start to believe in and accentuate your positives. Take time to learn to love yourself.

3. You Didn't Have Positive Roles Models

If one of your parents or primary caregivers didn't accept themselves, you may be modeling their behavior.

Antidote: find positive roles models now, people who love, accept and care for themselves with confidence. Follow their lead.

4. You've Made Self-Acceptance Conditional

You believe you need to achieve something before you can fully accept yourself. You're waiting to complete your education, earn a specific amount of money, or get a promotion at your job.

But even when you make it to a goal post, you find you still can't accept yourself. You tell yourself you need to reach the next before you do.

Antidote: take the conditions off and accept your whole self right, now.

5. You Are Trying To Live Up To Societal Norms

There's so much pressure to live up to societal norms within most families, at school, and in the advertisements that abound all around you.

You may not accept who you are because you think you should be someone else—the grade a student or the perfect mom and wife with the ideal figure and a corporate job too.

Antidote: break the societal norms! Make new ones! Make your own! Decide who you want to be for yourself.

6. Your Circle Is Not Supportive

It's difficult to feel good about yourself if your partner, friends, or employer are constantly putting you down. I know this for myself. I had a harsh boss for many years. His constant criticism eroded my self-confidence.

Antidote: surround yourself with people who love, appreciate, and support you, one person at a time. Leave unsupportive situations.

7. You've Been Traumatized

The experience of shock or early childhood trauma can trigger shame or the mistaken belief that you were somehow responsible.

Antidote: know this is a common reaction in trauma, but it doesn't make it true. Find a trauma therapist who can help you heal the trauma and transform these incorrect beliefs.

You can't go from zero self-acceptance to accepting yourself just like that. But it doesn't have to take eons either.

Positive repetition works overtime. It actually modifies your brain. Use these four steps to change your response:

1. "First, label the response you want to change."
2. "Second, identify the new response that you want to develop."
3. "Third, explore what factors might reduce the unwanted response and boost the desired response."
4. "Lastly, repeatedly practice the new response so that it becomes ingrained."

Start on the path of self-acceptance now. You'll feel very different in a few months and surely in a few years to come. You'll grow in self-love, self-acceptance, and your ability to care for yourself.

Won't that be so much better than rejecting yourself?

Chapter 9:

Stop Trying To Be Perfect

We're constantly given new advice on how to improve our lives. Meditate. Exercise. Get a hobby. Fast. Everything you do, from what you eat to how you spend your free time, seems like it can be optimized. Especially in the tech world, we're constantly striving toward making things better, ourselves included. It's no secret that running a startup changes your life. You want to make your company the best it can be the most efficient, innovative, and market leader. It's not surprising that the drive to improve bleeds into the rest of your life.

But self-improvement as a goal is ineffective. Are we trying to be perfect? And who defines what perfect is? It's so vague as to be unattainable. What if intermittent fasting makes you irritable? What if trying to fit one more thing in your day causes more stress than meditation alleviates? What if you hate kale? What if the "best" way to do things isn't the best way for you? If a goal is unachievable, what's the point in working towards it? It's true. We'll never reach perfection. At no point will we say, "I've reached the peak of who i can be. I can stop now."

But change will happen whether we control it or not. We, as people, are dynamic creatures. We keep growing and evolving throughout our whole lives. Striving for perfection is setting ourselves up for failure. But, by looking at our lives through the lens of self-improvement, we can be strategic about how we spend our time and energy. There is no one-size-fits-all solution. To be effective, we have to focus on personalized, specific changes.

Despite what the internet may tell you, it takes more than twenty minutes to change your life. It's a cumulative effect of daily or weekly work over a long period. And progress is not linear. As anyone who has built a company knows, there are peaks and valleys. Feeling like you do not see results can make it difficult to stick with a program.

Sometimes, self-improvement can feel impossible. You don't reach a goal and decide you're the best person you can be. It's an ever-evolving process. This can make the process frustrating. You're never done. It can be helpful to think of self-improvement as a practice more than an outcome, even if you do have specific goals you want to achieve. By trying to find enjoyment in work itself, you're more likely to stick with it in the long term.

For high achievers, self-improvement can feel like one more thing on an already full to-do list. Berating yourself for not sticking with a self-improvement plan can cause you to underestimate your potential, limiting your future development. Self-compassion can help encourage the growth mindset necessary for self-improvement. Self-compassion is treating yourself in the face of failure the way you would a good friend. By showing yourself kindness and understanding, you are investing in your wellbeing.

A growth mindset is a way of thinking in which people see their abilities as improvable rather than fixed. If you see your talents as static, why would you work to improve them? By encouraging a growth mindset, every day becomes a chance to get a little bit better. Perfection may be a myth. We will all always be works in progress. But, if we stay open to new experiences and learning opportunities, we give ourselves room to grow.

Chapter 10:

6 Tricks to Become More Aware Of Your Strengths

"Strength and growth come only through continuous effort and struggle." - Napoleon Hill.

While it is true that we tend to focus more on our weaknesses than on our strengths, it is also true that we should polish our strengths more than our weaknesses. This in no way means that we should consider ourselves superior to others and start looking away from that we have flaws. Unfortunately, most of us don't spend much time on self-reflection and self-awareness. But they are the vital aspects if we are thinking of improving ourselves in any way.

Here are 6 Tricks to become more aware of your strengths:

1. Decide To Be More Self-Aware

Human beings are complicated creatures. Our minds are designed so that we tend to absorb more negative than positive thoughts about ourselves and others. For this reason, self-awareness is perhaps the most crucial thing in an individual's life. Self-awareness is the ability to look deep inside of yourself and monitor your emotions and reactions. It is the ability to allow yourself to be aware of your strengths, weaknesses, as well as your triggers, motivators, and other characteristics. We'll help you find a set of tricks and techniques that you can apply to polish your strengths in a self-awareness way; and how to use your strengths in a promising way.

2. Meditation

The first thought that will come to your mind would be, "Is this person crazy? How can meditation help us improve our strengths?" But hear me out. The fresh breeze of the morning when everything is at peace, and you sit there inhaling all the good energy in and the bad energy out, your mind and thoughts would automatically become slow-paced and calm. Once you get to relax with yourself, you can analyze the things that have been happening in your life and develop possible solutions on how you can deal with them using your strengths. The positive energy and calming mood you will get after meditating would help you make your decisions wisely when you are under pressure and your mind is in chaos.

3. Labelling Your Thoughts

More often, our thoughts reflect on our behavior and what makes us fail or succeed in life. People can genuinely relate to a situation where they could have possibly thought about a worst-case scenario, but in the end, nothing as such happened. Our anxiety and hopelessness don't come from the situation we are struggling with, but rather our thoughts make us believe in the worst possible things that could happen to us. But we're stronger than we give ourselves credit for. We have the power to control our negative thoughts and turn them into positive ones. We can list all the ideas and thinking that provide us with stress and tension and then label them as either useful or useless. If the particular thought is causing a significant effect in your life, you can work towards it to make your life better and less anxious. Know your priorities and take help from your strengths to tackle the problems.

4. Befriending Your Fears

There's not a single person on this planet who isn't afraid of something. Be it the fear of losing your loved ones or any phobias of either animal, insects, heights, closed spaces, etc. There are also so many fears related to our self-worth and whether we are good enough, skilled enough, or deserving enough of anything. To accept these fears and work towards overcoming them is perhaps the most powerful thing one could do. It takes so much of a person's strength and willpower to befriend fear, reduce it, and finally eliminate it. Most of the time, we end up in situations that we always feared, and then we have to take quick actions and make wise decisions. To remain calm in such cases and use your strengths and experiences to tackle whatever's in front of you is a remarkable quality found in only a few. But we can also achieve and polish this quality by strengthening our minds and preparing ourselves to get us out of situations wisely and effectively. To be patient and look into the problems from every angle is the critical component of this one.

5. Watching Your Own Movie

Narrating your life experiences to yourself or a close friend and telling yourself and them how far you have come can boost your self-confidence immensely. You should go in flashbacks and try to remember all the details of your life. You will find that there were some moments you felt immense joy and some moments where you felt like giving up. But with all the strength that you were collecting along the way, you endured the possible tortures and struggles and challenges and eventually rose again. So you should focus and be well aware of how you tackle those situations, what powers you have, and the strengths that couldn't let you give up but face everything. Once you have found the answers to the above questions, like for example, it was your patience and bravery that helped you through it, or it was your wise and speedy decisions that made it all effective, you can understand what strengths you have and make use of them later in life too.

6. Motivate yourself

We should stop looking for others to notice how great we did or stop waiting for a round of applause or a pat on the back from them. Instead, we should motivate ourselves every time we fall apart, and we should have the energy to pick ourselves back up again. The feeling of satisfaction we get after completing a task or helping someone, that feeling is what we should strive for. We should become proud of ourselves and our strengths, as well as our weaknesses, that they helped us transform into the person we are today. We should never feel either superior or inferior to others. Everyone has their own pace and their own struggles. Our strengths should not only be for ourselves but for others too. Kindness, empathy, hospitality, being there for people, patience, courage, respect are all the qualities that one must turn into their strengths.

Conclusion

The key to perfection is self-awareness. There's a fine line between who you are and who you strive to become; it can be achieved by becoming aware of your strengths, polishing them, and creating a sense of professional as well as personal development. Your strengths motivate you to try new things, achieve new skills, become a better version of yourself. Your strengths are what keeps you positive, motivated, help you to maintain your stress better, aid you in your intuitive decision making, and command you to help others as well. It inspires you to become a better person.

Chapter 11:

Identifying Your Mission Statement

Self-Awareness

This is the take-off point if you ever want to identify your mission statement. It cannot be over-emphasized enough that you should 'discover' yourself before somebody else can understand you.

Self-awareness is to know what you stand for as a person and what you are willing to sacrifice for it. In self-awareness, you should know what your personal philosophy is that will make it easy to find your mission statement.

Personal Philosophy

It is the core values that drive your passion in life. Quite a handful of people have been able to realize this part of themselves. For example, some people believe that diplomacy can never solve an impasse. They will always resort to violence.

On the other hand, others believe entirely in diplomacy. They will always use it in problem-solving. These are two different categories of people with different philosophies, yet they aim to achieve the same goal.

The Process Of Identifying Your Mission Statement

After self-awareness and knowing your personal philosophy, you need to complete one more step. Self-audit.

Auditing is not a foreign concept. We know of companies' accounts being audited for transparency. Do the books of accounts observe correct accounting principles? Are all expenses backed up with matching purchase receipts and invoices?

This is financial auditing. You need to do the same with yourself. Self-auditing is reviewing your actions and intentions towards your philosophy. Know the areas in that you have performed well and those that you have not.

What Are Your Strengths?

It is important to know where you perform well as you live your personal philosophy. This is definitely where your personal philosophy lies.

Try to identify areas where you were praised for doing well. If other people recognized your excellence on something, focus on it. Therein lies your strength. Know the specific thing that you excelled in and continue working on it.

Using the same example of diplomacy and force to resolve a problem, what path did you choose when you faced a situation?
If you successfully made peace by diplomacy between conflicted parties, there it is! Peace-keeping is your mission statement.

What Are Your Weaknesses?

This is what lets you down even in your strongest moments. Like its name – weakness – you cannot overcome it alone no matter how hard you try.

Those around you could fault you for repeating the same mistake even after correction. As much as you could be willing to learn and get it right, you still need a lot of practice.

One thing we often forget is that we do not choose our weaknesses. It is like a default setting in us that we must continuously keep on turning off. You should never tire.

Our weaknesses make us human. None is perfect. In self-audit, you will work to improve your weakness because it is a danger to your mission statement.

What Are The Opportunities You Have?

You should know the chances allowing you to make it right coming your way as you live your personal philosophy. Your weaknesses could derail you or even take you off your path of destiny but the opportunities to make it right will present themselves every so often.

The earlier you identify opportunities like these, the better placed you are to seize them fully. Your mission statement is like a journey that comes with its challenges. There are rights, wrongs, and corrections. Opportunities are the chances you get to make corrections.

What Are The Threats You Face?

Enmity is not always lacking. Your mission statement is sometimes threatened with extinction. This can happen if you do not put measures in place to neutralize threats.

Threats could arise from weaknesses if they are not adequately addressed. Anger is such a weakness that threatens your mission statement if you do not work on it.

Consider your mission statement like a treasure that must be protected at all costs. Your life will lose direction if it is lacking.

Identifying your mission statement could be as easy as ABC but difficult if you do not follow through with this whole process fully. This is a call to action in the right direction.

Chapter 12:

How To Stop Lying To Ourselves: A Call For Self-Awareness

If you're serious about getting better at something, then one of the first steps is to know—in black-and-white terms—where you stand. You need self-awareness before you can achieve self-improvement.

Here are some tools I use to make myself more self-aware:

Workout Journal

For the past five years, I have used my workout journal to record each workout I do. While it can be interesting to leaf back through old workouts and see the progress I've made, I have found this method to be most useful every week. When I go to the gym next week, I will look at the weights I lifted the week before and try to make a small increase. It's so simple, but the workout journal helps me avoid wasting time in the gym, wandering around, and just "doing some stuff." With this basic tracking, I can make focused improvements each week.

Annual Reviews and Integrity Reports

At the end of each year, I conduct my Annual Review, where I summarize the progress I've made in business, health, travel, and other areas. I also take time each spring to do an Integrity Report where I challenge myself to provide proof of how I am living by my core values. These two practices give me a chance to track and measure the "softer" areas of my life. It can be difficult to know for certain if you're doing a better job of living by your values, but these reports at least force me to track these issues on a consistent basis.

A Call for Self-Awareness

If you aren't aware of what you're actually doing, then it is very hard to change your life with any degree of consistency. Trying to build better habits without self-awareness is like firing arrows into the night. You can't expect to hit the bullseye if you're not sure where the target is located.

Furthermore, I have discovered very few people who naturally do the right thing without ever measuring their behavior. For example, I know a handful of people who maintain six-pack abs without worrying too much about what they eat. However, every single one of them weighed and measured their food at some point. After months of counting calories and measuring their meals, they developed the ability to judge their meals appropriately.

In other words, measurement brought their levels of self-awareness in line with reality. You can wing it *after* you measure it. Once you're aware of what's actually going on, you can make accurate decisions based on "gut-feel" because your gut is based on something accurate.

In short, start by measuring something.

Chapter 13:

How To Be Your Own Best Friend

Why would you want to become your own best friend? There are several benefits to creating your internal support system rather than relying on your partner, friends, or family to be there for you when you're suffering. Having other people's expectations can lead to disappointment, heartbreak, and relationship breakdown if your expectations aren't met. We all have it in us to give ourselves what we need without seeking it externally.

Of course, it's great if you have a strong support network, but you could still benefit from becoming more self-reliant. And what about if you have no one to turn to for help, or if your current support people are unable to be there for you? Isn't it far better to know how to support yourself in times of need?

Here's how to become your own best friend.

1. Be Nice To Yourself

The first step to becoming a friend is to treat yourself like you would treat a friend. That means that you need to stop being self-critical and beating yourself up. Start by acknowledging your good qualities, talents, and abilities and begin to appreciate your unique self.

When you catch yourself thinking up some nasty self-talk, stop and ask, "Would I say this to my best friend?" If not, then reframe your self-talk to be more supportive and caring.

2. Imagine How You Would Support A Friend In The Same Situation

Think about a loved one, a friend, a family member, someone dear to you and imagine that they are in the same situation you are currently facing. Think about how they're struggling, suffering, and feeling stuck with this problem, then consider how to best offer assistance and advice to them.

Craft the words that you would say to your greatest friend and then say them gently to yourself. Allow yourself to feel supported and give yourself what you need.

3. Honor Your Needs

Following the theme of considering how you would help a dear friend, you need to start taking your advice and putting your own needs first. Do you need a day off from work? A long hot bath? An early night? A wild night? Some time to catch up on your reading, cleaning, gardening, creative projects, social life, or self-care?

Whatever you need, allow yourself to put it at the top of the list rather than the bottom. Be there for yourself and make it happen.

4. Send Compassion To The Part of You That is Hurting

Being a friend to yourself involves adopting and mastering the art of self-compassion. Compassion isn't forceful or solution focused. Compassion is accepting, peaceful, and loving, without the need to control or change anything.

Imagine a mother holding a child who has bumped his head. Her compassion is a strong force. She simply holds her child with loving, comforting, gentle arms and whispers, "It will be alright, my love." The child trusts his mother's words just as you learn to trust your own words when speaking to yourself.

Imagine yourself as both the child and the mother simultaneously. Offer compassion at the same time as you open up to receive it.

Use these techniques to become your own best friend and start *being there* for yourself!

Chapter 14:

How To Fight Worrying

The Good News

The good news in town is that you should stop worrying. Worry is a feeling of anxiety that stems from fear of failure. Our success is contributed by some factors that we may not have control over. It is unfair for us to judge ourselves harshly based on them.

Worrying will not change anything. We should focus on how we can change the situation instead of worrying about it. We try to meet the expectations that people have of us. The fear of letting them down is a cause of worry.

The Genesis Of Worrying

Worrying is caused by many other factors apart from the expectations of other people on us. We are afraid of letting ourselves down. Our history of failure could haunt us and we become uncertain whether we can change it.

Another cause of worry is the fear of the consequences of non-performance. We are afraid of what may befall us when we fail to succeed.

The genesis of constant worry could also come from childhood trauma. Experiences as children shape our adulthood. There could be no valid reason for us to worry but past experiences can make us always anxious.

All reasons for worrying are valid. It is a natural human feeling, but we should not allow it to overtake our mental stability.

Stop Worrying

There could be many reasons why you should worry but there are twice as much why you should not. Although worrying is a subconscious emotion that we hardly have control over, we can address the potential sources of worry. Here is how to:

1. Do Not Be A People-Pleaser

You cannot stop people from having expectations from you on anything. They can have their opinion about your ability and there is nothing you can do about it. However, do not live trying to impress them. You owe them nothing.

Continue pursuing your dreams without gauging yourself against their expectations. You will not strain and wear yourself out as you seek their approval. Prioritize your ambitions above their expectations and you will have nothing to worry about.

2. Be Self-Confident

Believe in yourself even when others doubt you. You will not worry about failure when you are self-confident. The greatest gift to yourself is trusting in your ability to deliver on your mandate. Do not worry about what you cannot control.

Worrying will pressure you to act wrongly. Delayed right action is better than a fast wrong move. Have the mental strength to withstand external pressure and believe in yourself.

3. Face Your Fears

Past trauma could indeed have a long-lasting impact on our adulthood. Our worry could be because of childhood abuse. We were punished when we could not perform and consequently developed performance anxiety.

Stop worrying because that ugly phase has passed. Fight performance anxiety by doing your best. Repeat what you were unable to do in childhood and succeed. You will no longer worry about it in the future.

4. Make A Move

If you can change something, why worry? Still, why worry if you cannot change it? This is a call to action. Worrying alone will change nothing. Do not despise your position. Make a bold move that you see can make things better.

Responsible adulting is proactive. Act without waiting on instructions. Your actions are for the greater good. There could be other people who have the same worry as you. It is a blessing when you make a move and assure them not to worry.

5. Look At The Brighter Side

Learn to look at the good side in every situation. There could be a reason why things are not moving as you expect. Your worry could be a deliberate act of nature for the greater good.

Looking at the brighter side will make you not worry about a lot of things. In due time, everything will work out as planned.

In conclusion, fighting worry is a deliberate decision that we make. Except we do it, no one will do it for you. These five ways will lead you out of worry.

Chapter 15:

Resist Temptations For Success

We all have hopes and dreams. We have a rough sketch of what we want to become and what we want to achieve. Most of us have good intentions for those things too.

But the reality is that process of achieving those things isn't always as simple as we all anticipate. It is all mixed up with all these temptations that are equally alluring and want us to give up everything else for just a moment and enjoy what we are about to indulge in.

You see if you were to make a milestone for a week where you were to lose a pound of weight with rigorous cardio and hours of strict training followed by a strict diet plan. You can't say you won't be tempted by the smell of fries and fried chicken whenever you walk past one.

Surely you would be OK, only if you resisted it and kept walking your way. But if you were to pick up one piece and put it in your mouth, you just destroyed the whole mantra of self-control and self-discipline.

Self-discipline is not just putting your life on track and following a timetable. Self-discipline is not punishing yourself for any mistake. Self-discipline is following a course of actions that will take you to your ultimate goal.

We all are susceptible to weaknesses. We often end up acting against the things and goals that we value the most.

Temptations are nature's way of testing us. It is a test to evaluate our core values and our integrity. It is a litmus test to pick the leaders out of a faction. Temptations are a way of self-analyzing ourselves whether we are worthy enough or are we still distracted with all the shiny things lying around.

It is easy to get a good grade with a little help from here and there. It is easy to follow someone else's path rather than carving our own. It is easier to fake some lab results to be enrolled into a team of representatives.

But when we get the chance to do those things in real life without any outside help on an open stage where the world is judging us, we cannot get ourselves to do any of those things because we cheated n the first place and never engaged the creative factory of our mind.

So how should you approach this problem? It is a simple step-by-step process.

Start by removing the temptations. Check for any loopholes in your environment and kick them out to keep them away long enough till you are more in control.

Next, you need to take some time to think about your way of thinking as an unbiased and nonhuman object. Try to find the flaws and reinvent them to disengage any magnets in your personality that keep attracting you to those temptations.

Last but not the least, put a zipper on your pocket and control your spending habits and you will get away from any unnecessary temptation leading you to a better successful life!

Chapter 16:

Six Habits of Self-Love

We can show gratitude to ourselves for our different achievements in many ways. It is something that most people overlook as a waste of time and resources. This is a fallacy. It is high time we develop habits of self-love, to recharge our bodies and minds in preparation for another phase of achievements.

Here are six habits of self-love:

1. Treating Yourself

It is showing gratitude to yourself by way of satisfying your deepest desires instead of waiting for someone else to do it for you. Take the personal initiative to go shopping and buy that designer suit or dress you have been wanting so badly. Do not wait for someone else to do it for you while you are capable.

Take that much-needed vacation and a break from work to be with your family. Spend time with the people you love and cherish every moment because, in this fast-moving world, the future is uncertain. Secure your happiness lest you drown in depression. The best person to take care of your interests is yourself.

Who will take you out for swimming or outing to those posh hotels if you do not initiate it? Self-love begins when you realize your worth and do not allow anyone else to bring it down.

2. Celebrate Your Victories

Take advantage of every opportunity to celebrate your wins, no matter how small. A habit of self-love is to celebrate your achievements and ignore voices that discourage you. Nothing should muffle you from shouting your victories to the world. The testimony of your victory will encourage a stranger not to give up in his/her quest.

It is neither pride nor boastfulness. It is congratulating yourself for the wins that you rightfully deserve. How else can you love yourself if you do not appreciate yourself for the milestones you have conquered? Do not shy away from thanking yourself, privately or publicly, because no one else best knows your struggles except yourself.

3. Accept Yourself

To begin with, accept your social and economic status because you know the battles you have fought. Self-acceptance is an underrated form of self-love. Love yourself and accept your shortcomings. When you learn to accept yourself, other people will in turn accept you. They will learn how to accommodate you in the same manner you learned to live with all your imperfections.

Self-loathing dies when you master self-acceptance and self-love. Self-care keeps off self-rejection. You begin seeing your worth and great potential. It is the enemy within that is responsible for the fall of great empires.

The enemy within is low self-esteem and self-rejection. Accept the things you cannot change and change the things in your ability. Do not be hard on yourself because a journey of a thousand miles begins with a single step.

4. Practice Forgiveness

Forgiveness is a strong act. When you forgive those who wrong you, you let go of unnecessary baggage. It is unhealthy to live with a heart full of hate (pun intended). Forgiveness does not mean that you have allowed other people to wrong you repetitively. It means you have outgrown their wrong acts and you no longer allow their inconsiderate acts to affect you. Forgiveness benefits the forgiver more than the forgiven. It heals the heart from any hurt caused. It is the best form of self-care yet difficult at the same time. Forgiveness is a gradual process initiated by the bigger person in any conflict. Practicing self-care is by recognizing the importance of turning a new leaf and staying free from shackles of grudges and bitterness.

Unforgiveness builds bitterness and vengeance. It finally clouds your judgment and you become irrational. Choosing forgiveness is a vote on self-care.

5. Choose Your Associates Wisely

Associate with progressive people. Show me your friends and I will tell you the kind of person you are. Your friends have the potential to either build or destroy your appreciation of self-worth. They will trim your excesses and supplement your deficiencies. A cadre of professionals tends to share several traits.

Self-care involves taking care of your mental state and being selective of who you let into your personal space. It supersedes all other interests.

6. Engaging In Hobbies

Hobbies are the activities we do during our free time to relax our minds and bond with our friends. When doing these hobbies we are at ease and free from pressures of whatever form. We need to take a break from our daily work routine from time to time and do other social activities.

Hobbies are essential to explore other interests and rejuvenate our psyche and morale. Self-love places your interests and well-being above everything else. There is a thin line between it and selfishness, but it is not the latter.

These six habits of self-love will ensure you have peace and sobriety of mind to make progressive decisions.

Chapter 17:

Signs You are Bottling Up Your Emotions

An Airtight Bottle

People are like big bottles that can store anything. There are a million ways you can be useful and have a bigger impact on the people around you. Along the same line, we develop emotions from how we interact with people. So, what does it mean when you bottle up your emotions?

To bottle up your emotions means to shut down yourself from other people. It extends to not sharing your feelings with them for various reasons. People with different personality traits have different approaches to bottling up their emotions.

The Influence of Personality Traits

While extroverts prefer making their lives public, introverts have a hard time doing the same. Different personality traits inform the decision people take to share their emotions too much, a little, or not at all. Previous experiences have a role too in whether you are ready to open up. Emotions make us vulnerable to the person we are confiding in. You will understand why some people take forever before deciding whether or not to confide in someone.

Here are some of the reasons you may be bottling up your emotions:

1. The Need For Peace

Everybody wants peace. You want to have some quiet time alone without anyone bothering you about this or that. This makes you decide to keep things to yourself because sharing it may cause unnecessary drama. There are some people who feel entitled to your life. They want to know every bit of it and it will be a cold day in hell if you share emotions with them that are contrary to their wishes. The best thing is to hold your peace and bottle up your emotions.

2. Low Self-Esteem

Another reason you could be bottling up your emotions is low self-esteem. It makes you feel worthless and undeserving of other people's attention and love. This could not be the case because the people you think you are bothering with your emotions are more than happy to listen to you. People with higher self-esteem mostly open up without any fear of how other people will think about them. Make no mistake, some people have high self-esteem and are introverted. They hardly open up about what they are feeling. It has nothing to do with low self-esteem. It is their personality.

3. Fear Of Judgment

What happened the last time you opeed up could be the reason you are bottling up your emotions. You would rather keep things to yourself than face public judgment from people who feel entitled to your life. People will always talk and there is nothing you can do about it. It is up to you to be yourself and live a life devoid of their influence.

Signs You are Bottling Up Your Emotions

1. Withdrawal

You should be concerned if you or someone you know withdraws from people every single time. Withdrawal means that you want nothing to do with them probably because of them being judgmental or your search for inner peace. While it can be a good thing in the present, in the long term, it can affect how you relate with other people.

2. Agreeing With Everyone On Everything

Quickly agreeing about something is a red flag. It could indicate that you are not ready to engage them further. It could also point out that you are bottling up your emotions because of low self-esteem. Rational people debate over an issue before agreeing to it. It is okay to agree without question but doing it every time is a cause for worry.

3. Frequent Anger Outbursts Over Small Matters

This is the beginning of a breakdown for people who bottle up their emotions. They manage to do it for some time until they no longer continue with it. It manifests in their frequent anger outburst and they could end up in depression. Anger is a normal emotion but at the tip of it, it could be a sign that you are bottling up your emotions.

4. Talking To Yourself

This is mostly the case if you have no one to talk to. Most peole think that people who talk to themselves have a mental illness but this is not always true. You could talk to yourself because you have no one to talk to (or rather you prefer not to talk to anyone). Talking to yourself becomes the only outlet to manage your emotions.

Emotional Intelligence

In conclusion, emotional intelligence will help you to effectively manage your emotions. Emotions are not entirely bad. You can use them to channel your energy to one place and hit your target. Bottling up your emotions, on the contrary, is like covering a fire. There will be smoke and eventually what you are using to cover the fire will burn.

Chapter 18:

How To Live Authentically

What does being authentic mean? How do I know if the life I'm leading is authentic? Am I happy with the person I've become? Finally, is authenticity overrated? And if you're anything like me, your train of thought maybe similar. It's easy to forget how to be authentic when we play many different roles throughout the day. We're parents, children, friends, employees, teachers, lovers, members of society. But how do we stay true to ourselves when life gets messy, overwhelming, or stressful?

By taking small steps and doing little things that make us feel good. No, scratch that. That makes us feel great. Excellent. Ecstatic. Alive. Grateful for who we are and what we have. But also calm, meditative, reflective. I made a shortlist of simple things that have helped me live more authentically and be closer to my genuine self.

1. Enjoy The Little Things

I know – this is a cliché, but I can't deny this simple truth. In all honesty, it can take some practice to train your mind to stop blabbering and start noticing the little things. But once it does, you will. Rejoice in the first rays of sunshine on a hazy morning. Feel their warmth on your skin.

Smell that first cup of coffee and exhale with a sigh of blissful pleasure as you take that first sip. Hug your pet. Kiss your loved one. Have fresh flowers on your table. Listen to the ocean. Watch the sunset. Let the wind blow through your hair in the spring. Walk on crispy leaves in the fall.

Make snow angels in the winter. You know, the little things. Every day, I make conscious efforts to appreciate and remember the special moments and people in my life.

2. Don't Judge or Punish Yourself For Your Mistakes

We often think it's ok to judge ourselves for a mistake we've made either now or in the past. But what's the use? Instead of beating yourself up, see if you can learn something from your failures. So, what helps is writing down what each of your mistakes is trying to teach you and how you can avoid repeating it in the future. But please, don't judge yourself. You did the best you could do.

Sometimes, you'll find your true self with life experience and maturity. Other times, it may be hidden under anxiety and depression, feelings of inadequacy, negative self-talk, self-doubt, and fear. And finding it may take some therapy. But the authentic self has no high expectations of themselves or others and takes life lightly. Instead of constantly doing, running, working, thinking – it *just is*. Innocent and vulnerable, but also strong and independent. For me, *authenticity equals freedom*.

So, tell me – what does authenticity mean to you? How do you find it? Do you have any tips to add to this list? I'd love to hear your thoughts in the comments below.

Chapter 19:

What To Do When You Feel Like Your Work is not Good Enough

Feeling like your work is not good enough is very common; your nerves can get better of you at any time throughout your professional life. There is nothing wrong with nerves; It tells you that you care about improving and doing well. Unfortunately, too much nervousness can lead to major self-doubt, and that can be crippling. You are probably very good at your work, and when even once you take a dip, you think that things are not like how they seem to you. If this is something you're feeling, then you're not alone, and this thing is known as Imposter Syndrome. This term is used to describe self-doubt and inadequacy. This one thing leaves people fearing that there might be someone who will expose them. The more pressure you apply to yourself, the more dislocation is likely to occur. You create more anxiety, which creates more fear, which creates more self-doubt. You don't have to continue like this. You can counter it.

Beyond Work

If your imposter syndrome affects you at work, you should take some time out and start focusing on other areas of your life. There are chances that there is something in your personal life that is hindering your work life. This could be anything your sleep routine, friends, diet, or even your relationships. There is a host of external factors that can affect your performance. If there are some boxes you aren't ticking, then there is a high chance of you not performing well at work.

You're Better Than You Think

When you're being crippled by self-doubt, the first thing you have to think about is why you were hired in the first place. The interviewers saw something in you that they believed would improve the business.

So, do you think they would recruit someone who can't do the job? No, they saw your talent, they saw something in you, and you will come good. When you find yourself in this position, take a moment to write down a few things that you believe led to you being in the role you are now. What did those recruiters see? What did your boss recognize in you? You can also look back on a period of time where you were clicking and felt victorious. What was different then versus now? Was there an external issue like diet, exercise, socializing, etc.?

Check Yourself Before You Wreck Yourself

A checklist might be of some use to you. If you have a list to measure yourself against, then it gives you more than just one thing to judge yourself against. We're far too quick to doubt ourselves and criticize harshly.

The most obvious checklist in terms of work is technical or hard skills, but soft skills matter, too. It's also important to remember that while you're technically proficient now, things move quickly, and you'll reach a point where everything changes, and you have to keep up. You might not ever excel at something, but you can accept the change and adapt to the best of your ability.

It matters that you're hard-working, loyal, honest, and trustworthy. There's more to judge yourself on than just your job. Even if you make a mistake, it's temporary, and you can fix it.

Do you take criticism well? Are you teachable? Easy to coach? Soft skills count for something, which you can look to even at your lowest point and recognize you have strengths.

When you're struggling through a day, week, or even a month, take one large step backward and think about what it is you're unhappy with. What's causing your unhappiness, and how can you improve it?

It comes down to how well you know yourself. If you're clear on what your values are and what you want out of life, then you're going to be fine. If the organization you work for can't respect your values and harness your strengths, then you're better off elsewhere. So, it is extremely important to take time out for that self check-in there could be times you talk to yourself in negative light. Checking in with yourself regularly and not feeding yourself negativity could be one-step forward.

Chapter 20:

How To Use Military Strategy To Build Better Habits

What Is The Military?

Every country has a military. It is tasked with the duty of protecting the country's borders against external aggression and at times it quells internal violence or gets involved in rescue missions, both internally and externally. The men and women in uniform have a higher calling to serve and protect. Regardless of the nation they serve, they all have a common code of conduct they abide by.

Military Training

From recruitment to the hiring of personnel, military training is a serious affair. It is tough and no-nonsense. Their training is not limited to building their physical agility but also fortifying their mental strength and strategizing skills. They are trained through the most difficult situations and terrains and taught to withstand extremely harsh conditions.

Military strategies are full proof with almost zero chances of failure because they implement them to the latter or else they will have to pay with their lives on the battlefield. We can use such strategies to build better habits for ourselves and future generations.

Here are ways to use military strategies to build better habits:

1. Discipline

The military is also called the disciplined force because their discipline is unmatched. There is a clear hierarchy of protocol on who can issue what orders. There is no option of questioning orders from above; only their enforcement. Such streamlined command is lacking in the civilian world.

Ironically, democracies are chaotic even when they are expected to be orderly because the majority have their say. This tendency makes progress slow and nothing can thrive. Good habits cannot blossom to bear fruits and the existing ones suffer a natural death.

At a personal level, uphold undemocratic military discipline if you want to succeed in building better habits. This kind of discipline acknowledges order and does not give room for action only when it is convenient. It is unpopular but functional.

Resolve to work on goals you had set without allowing excuses to slow you down. Be reasonable but ruthless in enforcing boundaries and work towards your goals. This is the type of military discipline that has been tried, tested, and proved to be working.

2. Timekeeping

Lack of punctuality has punctured the wheels of a majority of people. It is a chronic disease in our lives but the military has found its cure. Observe timeliness like your life depends on it. Punctuality will open doors you never knew existed in the first place. You build a reputation of a person possessing a rare quality – punctuality.

Broken promises, disappointments, unemployment, and missed business deals have partly been a product of lateness. We have disappointed the people we love and prospective business partners because we failed in keeping time.

The military knows better that timekeeping can save lives and seal the success of a mission. This is a strategy they have perfected. Instilling it in your life will create room to allow other positive habits to grow in your lives. Timeliness will make you stand out in this competitive world of slim chances.

3. Physical Agility

Physical agility is beyond appearance. It is a strategy that will ensure you fit in places where a majority of people do not. You will be flexible to run errands fast, and not get exhausted easily. It is difficult to find a physically unfit military officer. They are always in shape for them not to be a burden to their colleagues during training or on the battlefield.

It is a principal feature sought after in recruits. This strategy is a fertile ground for the development of better habits like exercising. The benefits of keeping fit to outweigh any inconveniences that you may encounter.

Other better habits like nutrition will be perfected if you work on physical agility. You will be physically fit if you have proper feeding habits. Military officers eat well-cooked balanced meals free of junk. This habit keeps them healthy and fit.

4. Planning

Planning is the master strategy because everything depends on it. A good plan is a job half done and the military knows better not to skip it. The enemy can have an undue advantage over soldiers with a weak plan or one full of loopholes. They will easily win in a war against a military starved of a solid plan. This makes it paramount to have a water-tight plan crafted beforehand and checked for anything not anticipated to be included.

Planning is a managerial function but the military has perfected it as a strategy mainly because their survival in war is dependent on how solid their plan is. You will not fall into bankruptcy if you plan well for your finances. Nobody wants to be a financial parasite on other people. Cure this with military-style planning.

Life is akin to a game of chess; one wrong move and you are at checkmate. You will build better spending, learning, and working habits if you plan your life properly. Look at the bigger picture before making key decisions lest you regret it when it is too late.

5. Self-control

How many times have you acted out of anger or happiness? Self-control is a trait that most civilians lack. We all have acted out of our emotions at one point. We vowed not to do one thing or another yet found ourselves back at it after a little while. This is caused by a lack of self-control.

Military training is where you are taught to detach yourself from your emotions. You instead reason with your mind, not your heart. This strategy has enabled officers to make reasonable decisions for the greater good of the team.

When a man can control his appetite for anything, he wields a lot of power. Many people lack self-control and they go ahead to satisfy their temporary gratifications. They end up losing all the gains they had made.

It is possible to master self-control and act only when the time is right. The military does it and so can you. Take a cue from them.

In conclusion, better habits cannot be built from anywhere. They need to have a strong foundation. Military strategies are full proof and the best foundation you could get.

Chapter 21:

How To Stop Getting In Your Own Way

Are there valid reasons why you can't get things done? Absolutely. In fact, many times, external forces are working against you — think a sick child, flat tire, or global pandemic. There are, however, times when it turns out that we're our own biggest obstacle. We also call this self-sabotage. And, it can be brutal when it comes to productivity and our wellbeing. The good news? You can conquer this by getting out of your way. And, it's feasible by trying out the following techniques.

Remember Your Why

Instead of going through the motions and doing things for no reason, reconnect with your purpose. If you can't connect the dots between the activity and the big picture, then stop doing it. That doesn't mean avoiding tasks that you don't always enjoy. For example, as a new business owner, you might dread bookkeeping. However, it's an essential responsibility if you want your business to thrive. Remind yourself that maintaining your finances, sticking to a budget, and preparing your taxes can help you reach your business goals. And, as your business scales up, you can eventually hand this off to someone else.

Acknowledge Your Strengths

A strength is an activity that strengthens you. It doesn't have to be something that you excel at. Instead, it's something that you look forward to and "leaves you feeling energized. A strength is more appetite than ability, and it's that appetite that drives us to want to do it again; practice more; refine it to perfection. The appetite leads to the practice, which leads to performance. Leveraging your strengths and managing around your weaknesses isn't just about making yourself feel better. It's about conditioning yourself to contribute the best of yourself every day. It's about performance.

Nothing Compares To You — Except You

You bust your tail but aren't as productive as a colleague. You see that a friend just bought a new car or are enjoying a luxurious vacation. And, that just leaves you feeling like a failure. But, as Mark Twain once said, "comparison is the death of joy." Research backs that statement up. Comparing yourself to others leads to low self-confidence and depression. It can also make you green with envy, deplete motivation, and doesn't bring you closer to your goals. In short, if you measure yourself against others, you're always going to come short. Instead, practice gratitude. And, better yet, compare yourself by tracking your progress and celebrating what you've accomplished.

Run With the Right Crowd

Are you familiar with saying, "you are what you eat?" "Well, it's also true when it comes to who you keep company with. You may not realize this. But, the people you interact with on a daily basis directly influence who you are and what you do. Make sure you surround yourself with people who encourage you and hold you accountable—people from who you can learn positive habits from.

Remove Unnecessary Pressure

Life is hectic enough. So, why make things worse by overcommitting or setting unrealistic expectations? Be realistic about what you can actually accomplish. If you don't have the availability or skillset, just say "no." For example, if you're calendar is already packed, decline time requests like unnecessary meetings or talking to a friend on the phone for two hours.

Engage In Self-Care

Some might consider self-care as a selfish act. In reality, it's making time for activities that leave you feeling calm and energized. These are vital in supporting your mental, physical, and emotional wellbeing. Examples can include going for a walk, journaling, hobbies, meditating, or taking a shower. Since time might appear to be a concern, add self-care to your calendar. For instance, you could leave an hour blank from 1 pm to 2 pm to spend however you like.

Avoid Ruminating

Ruminating is a cycle of repeating thoughts that you just can't shake. As a result, this can impair thinking and problem-solving. And, it can cause you to get stuck in your own head. To break free of these swirling thoughts, distract yourself. Examples are doing chores, reading, or calling a friend. You can also question your beliefs, set more attainable goals, and take small action steps to solve problems.

Chapter 22:

Plan A Trip For Happiness

This past year has been difficult as the COVID-19 pandemic has impacted everyone around the world in a different way. Taking precaution with social-distancing and self-isolation measures, people have had to search for unique ways to find moments of peace and happiness. While there have been many obstacles to overcome, in my own home we have found joy in the little moments like having extra time for self-care and starting new family traditions that foster creativity and bonding. One unexpected part of "normal life" that many people are missing right now is leisure travel.

Travel has the unique ability to transform lives by allowing us to become immersed in new cultures, gain a deeper understanding of ourselves, and a greater appreciation for life, and of course, experience an elevated level of happiness along the way. After returning home from exploring a far-flung destination, or even one that's nearby, I always feel a renewed sense of self and find more joy in the day-to-day moments of my personal life. While not everyone feels comfortable traveling yet, now is a great time to plan a future trip as a fun way to increase overall happiness by connecting with family members and enjoying the anticipation of an upcoming, big activity.

Recent Hilton research uncovered that nearly 9 out of 10 travellers agree that their travel memories are some of the happiest ones of their lives. The act of traveling creates lifelong, happy memories that people treasure and revisit often, more so than all other types of memories collected over the years. But 95% of those who travel are missing vacationing right now. What's even more concerning is that we're facing a travel memory deficit with 188 million travellers feeling there is a lack of travel memories being created. This, combined with widespread health concerns, means vacationing isn't an option for most right now.

However, all is not lost. Beyond the many upcoming scientific and societal advancements that lead experts to believe travel will soon be possible again, the simple act of planning a trip can greatly increase happiness and help fill the void the lack of travel has left so many of us with. A recent study conducted by the Institute for Applied Positive Research found that 97% of respondents report that having a trip planned makes them happier. While planning is certainly a different kind of happiness than physically going on a vacation, the process of finding the perfect route, accommodations and activities can be a temporary distraction from the difficult times we're going through. Additionally, the anticipation and sense of hopefulness for better times can keep us motivated and excited for the delayed gratification of a getaway. This "light at the end of the tunnel" often has a long-term mood-boosting effect and can help us relax as it puts us in the mind frame of a more soothing future.

Beyond the psychological benefits planning a vacation can provide, it's a great time to book as many travel options are less expensive right now, and travel companies have increased flexibility in terms of moving dates and cancelations. Companies are also going above and beyond to prioritize cleanliness to give guests complete peace of mind.

While we have an uncertain road ahead of us in terms of a return to normal travel, starting to think about where we want to go next can be a positive exercise in lifting our spirits and fostering mental well-being.

Chapter 23:

The People You Need in Your Life

We all have friends, the people that are there for us and would be there no matter what. These people don't necessarily need to be different, and these traits might all be in one person. Friends are valuable. You only really ever come across ones that are real. In modern-day society, it's so hard to find friends that want to be your friends rather than just to use you.

Sometimes the few the better, but you need some friends that would guide you along your path. We all need them, and you quite possibly have these traits too. Your friends need you, and you may not even know it.

1. The Mentor

No matter which area or field they are trying to excel in, the common denominator is that they have clarity about life and know exactly what their goals are. These people can impact you tremendously, helps you get into the winners' mindset, infuse self-belief and confidence in you then you, too, can succeed and accomplish your goals. They act as a stepping stone for you to get through your problems. They are happy for your success and would guide you through the troubles and problems while trying to get there.

2. Authentic People

You never feel like you have to make pretense around these people. Life can be challenging enough, so having friends that aren't judging you and are being themselves is very important for your well-being. This type of friend allows you to be vulnerable, express your emotion in healthy ways, and helps bring a smile back to your face when you're down.

They help you also show your true self and how you feel. Rather than showing only a particular side of their personality, they open their whole self to you, allowing you to do the same and feel comfortable around them.

3. Optimists

These people are the kind you need, the ones that will encourage you through tough times. They will be there encouraging you, always seeing the best in the situation. Having the ability to see the best in people and will always have an open mind to situations. Everyone needs optimism in their lives, and these people bring that.

"Optimism is essential to achievement, and it is also the foundation of courage and true progress." -Nicholas M. Butler.

4. Brutally Honest People

To have a balanced view of yourself and be aware of your blind spots is important for you. Be around people who would provide authentic feedback and not sugarcoat while giving an honest opinion about you. They will help you be a better version of yourself, rectifying your mistakes, work on your weak spots, and help you grow. These are the people you can hang around to get better, and you will critique yourself but in a good way, helping you find the best version of yourself. Of course, the ones that are just rude should be avoided, and they should still be nice to you but not too nice to the point where they compliment you even when they shouldn't.

Chapter 24:

Motivate Yourself

Motivation is a multibillion dollar industry.

There are many great motivational materials to help keep you motivated.

Some of the motivational material is great and should be studied and applied but this kind of motivation is what I call push, which is a good start, but in combination with pull motivation, (your personal why and reason), you can reach your goals faster.

With the use of videos, books, audio material and concentrating on your reasons, the sky really is the limit.

Using what works for you, which may be different than what works for others.

Motivation is very much personal to you.

Work with what pulls you and pushes you to reach your goals on record time.

Pushing and pulling everyday until your dream becomes reality.

The pull is your WHY , the big reason for taking action in the first place.

The pull is the motivations that effect you personally, and the big fire that will help your dream burn, even through the storms and the rain. Using the push motivators in conjunction to maximize your motivation on all fronts.

Create as much of your dream around you as you can with what you have right now to make it seem more real.
Pictures, music, videos, foods, smells , clothing.
Whatever you can do to create it now.

The engine to drive you there may not have arrived yet, but don't close the factory, work on the interior and bodywork, because your engine is on the way.
You know what you want, you know the first steps, take them in confidence, not fear.
If the dream is here, it is already real if you just believe and move towards it.

With motivation, self-determination and faith you have already won the race before it has even begun.
Setting up the ideal environment for the garden of your life to flourish.
Strengthen the desire, strengthen the belief.

Motivation in the mind without belief in the heart will only lead to disappointment.
Your why must be something close to the heart for you to endure the tribulations of champions.

Your motivations must be clear and personal.

Defining your purpose, often money alone will not make us happy.

The money must have a greater personal purpose to bring you happiness.

Giving often feels more rewarding than receiving.

As living a truthful life is more rewarding than deceiving.

The key to your dreams is often what you are believing.

Believing in yourself and your capabilities is key.

You can study every bit of motivational material ever made, but if you don't believe in yourself, you cannot be successful.

Self-belief and self-motivation are far stronger than the push of what we can learn from the outside.

Let the outside information light the fire as it is intended, be a keen learner of what is relevant, and motivate yourself by concentrating on what is important to you.

Motivate yourself, health, happiness and wealth.

It's possible for you now.

If you believe and push to achieve.

Chapter 25:

Building Confidence

The things we strive for all our lives are a mere image of what we can achieve and what we want to achieve.

There is a difference between two very important aspects of our life. One is self-esteem and the other is self-confidence. You have very high self-esteem if you think big of yourself and have respect for your craft. This is a very important thing to have because no one is big on confidence if they don't have a good opinion about themselves.

We often say that 'You and You only are your best critic'. This isn't a statement for the narrow-minded.

If you think big of yourself, you will have a better perspective of the things you do and wish to do someday. If you have a 'No Go' confidence towards everything, then you have nothing to start with.

Do you want to build confidence? Take some tips, just as a piece of advice.

If you want to build confidence, focus on what you can't do, not on what you can't. I know this is against everything we think someone will say to boost your morale.

But the truth is, that when you start to work on things that you cannot do, you will try it for some time, but then you will eventually fail. That might prove to be a breaking point for some people.

If you focus on what you can do, you will always be successful. And you will praise your good work, and that will help you every time exponentially. The more you proceed, the more you will succeed and the more you will be confident in yourself.

You also need to surround yourself with people who believe in you.

Every person in his life has had a moment when they were just about to summit the biggest achievement of their life. But gave up or lost hope because they let the noise and opinions around them get into their heads.

Those who have opinions have nothing else going on in their lives. So, they try to mend their souls by inflicting negation on others. You don't have time or energy to deal with these people.

So, keep the people in your life who have the same approach towards life as you and they love you for who you are. These people will help you in even the darkest deepest days of your life.

The last piece of advice is what we have heard from the first step that we took in our childhood. The advice of never giving up!

You will fail here and there everywhere in your life. You are meant to fail. Everyone is meant to fail someday. But you cannot give up! You Should Never Give Up!

We have a lot of things going on in our lives and one or the other is meant to fall apart someday. We lose money. We lose friends. We lose family. But what you cannot lose forever is Hope.

Till the day you have hope, you have a reserve to keep you on the track and maybe someday, fly like a phoenix.

Chapter 26:

Never Stop Even If Someone Tells You To

Your brain works in mysterious ways, and it has a way of complying with negative things much faster than the positives. It is a part of human nature to not accept things that make one feel good about themselves because if they do, they are termed "narcissistic" or "self-obsessed."

With the way things have taken a turn, the world has become a much more competitive place, and one needs to shoot for the moon to land among the stars. In a world so fast, if you can come up with unique and different ideas from others, not only do you stand out, but it also gives rise to the opposition. This is where people start discouraging you and telling you how you are not good enough. This is where your idea gets lost in their judgment, and you start doubting yourself and question if everything is worth it or not.

A million people out there are ready to step on you and crush your self-esteem and confidence because that is what they strive for. If you give them the strength and ability to take that away from you, it is in your hands. One of the strongest weapons one has is self-confidence which can take them to places they had only dreamt of, but if it is crushed, all that is ahead is failure and insecurities. As Johann Wolfgang von Goethe said, "As soon as you trust yourself, you will know how to live."

The path of success is never doubting yourself when someone tells you "No" and moving forward by trusting yourself instead of putting it in their judgment. If people's opinions measured success, great people like Albert Einstein wouldn't have made history. He failed school at the age of 16 and was told that he would always be a failure but imagine if he had stopped then, who would have developed the theory of relativity? Probably no one!

The truth is that while you might be good in one thing, you will always lack in one thing or another and you will be made felt like you are a failure. It is important not to listen to people when they tell you to stop because you cannot do it. You can! And you should not believe otherwise. Imagine if Einstein was asked to write a love song? Or Rihanna to come up with a theory of relativity? We wouldn't have had a world-class singer or a physicist. Thus, it is important to figure out your strengths and work towards polishing them. Move on with things and put in that belief that you can do it. Because trust us, if you tell yourself, you can do it. No one telling you otherwise will matter!

Chapter 27:

How To Stop Judging Your Own Work

Have you been extra nice to yourself lately? If you're a writer ... the answer is probably: "...mayyyybe?"

Writers — creators in general — are way too hard on themselves. We like making things, and we feel good doing it. But we really want to feel like we're doing a good job.

When we don't feel that way — which happens much more often than we realize — we start to doubt if writing is even worth the struggle. Why are we so judgmental of our own work? Because it's the easiest to judge. It comes from us. We know it better than anyone.

But we can all learn to be critical without being so harsh. Here's how. Remind yourself that not everything you write is going to feel polished. And the simple reason for that? The majority of the time, it won't be.

You have to make messes to make masterpieces. You have to do things wrong, you have to not do your best if you're ever going to learn what you're actually capable of. If what you're writing seems terrible — well, it might be. That doesn't mean it always will be, or that it will be the best thing you'll ever write.

You're going to write sentences you're unsure of, paragraphs that just don't "sound quite right." You're going to question whether or not this scene should stay or go. You're going to ask yourself a million times if you're doing any of this right.

What matters most is that you keep writing anyway. You can't polish something unfinished. Even if a draft feels like the worst thing you've ever written, at least you have something to work with — something you can improve little by little until it meets your personal standards (if that's even possible ...).

Focus on how you feel about your work, not on how others might react. We're all guilty of imagining how our future readers will react to certain parts of our stories. Sometimes, it's what keeps you going when you're starting to feel unsure. When you laugh at your own writing (admit it — it happens to you too), you picture others laughing too.

But there's a dark side to this train of thought. If we focus too much on what people might think about our writing, we can begin to worry that they won't like it. That they'll tell everyone else not to read it. That our words aren't actually good ... that they never will be.

The best way to judge whether or not your writing is meaningful and readable is if it feels that way to you. Yes, your readers matter whether they exist yet or not. You are writing for their entertainment. But until you get your words in front of eyes, the only opinion that matters is yours.

Your inner critic will never stop talking, but you can tune it out. Here's the truth not every writing expert will tell you: you will never stop doubting or judging yourself or your writing. There is no magic cure for self-criticism. But that doesn't mean you can't tone it down enough to avoid letting it interfere with your work.

We judge ourselves more harshly than everyone else does (even though it sometimes feels the other way around) because we genuinely want to do a good job. And deep down we know we are the only ones in control of whether or not we do the work "well."

The problem is, we're so used to seeing others' work and the kinds of writing that gets high praise that we often can't help but compare our drafts to their published masterpieces. When we do that, our writing just never feels "as good." We immediately spiral into "i'll never be good enough" self-talk. We get sad. We stop writing.

That negative self-talk will always be there. You will always hear it.
But you don't have to listen to it.
You don't have to care about the lies it's telling you. You don't have to let them stop you from doing the work you know you're meant to do.

It's one thing to say you're not going to pay attention to your voice of doubt and another to actually ignore it. It's not that simple for a lot of people — and that's ok. Some have an easier time quieting their minds than others. As a writer, it's often one of those things you learn to do the longer you do it, the more you practice it.

That voice in your head telling you that you'll never achieve your dreams?

The best thing you can do to demote its scream to a whisper is to prove it wrong.

Chapter 28:

3 Ways To Master Your Next Move

"I don't know what to do with my life!" If you find yourself saying this, you're not alone. It's common for people to get to a point where they feel stuck or directionless. It can result from poor decision making or an inability to make decisions at all.

This state of not knowing what to do next applies to a lot of people, at any age and at different times in your life.

Personally, I have discovered that following these 5 steps will help you to find out what to do with your life, feel good, and get unstuck.

1. Get Moving and Clear Your Mind

"Not knowing what you want is a lot better than knowing exactly what you want but not being able to get it, at least you have hope."

I once faced a very challenging and emotional time; all I could do was think about what I needed to do to get to the next day.

There were no thoughts of what I wanted to do in the future nor were there any thoughts of how I wanted my life to be. It was just a matter of surviving from one day to the next.

For me, during this challenging time, when I was telling myself, "I don't know what to do with my life," exercise was the solution to helping me get through my day.

Every morning my alarm would go off at 6 am. I would have my running gear ready by the bed. I would get dressed, walk out the door, and start running for 45 minutes.

For a long time, it was hard to get out of bed and go for my run because I just wanted to hide away. Over time, I began to look forward to my morning run as I felt more energized, and I was sleeping better.

2. Wake Your Conscious Mind and Limit Choices

"Nobody is going to do your life for you. You have to do it yourself, whether you're rich or poor, out of money or making it, the beneficiary of ridiculous fortune or terrible injustice…Self pity is a dead end road. You can make the choice to drive down it. It's up to you to decide to stay parked there or to turn around and drive out." -Cheryl Stryed.

116

Life isn't predictable, and the solutions we seek to answer our life questions don't always come nicely wrapped. There are no rules to follow, and you have to work hard to define your life pathway when you don't know what to do with your life.

Waking our conscious minds to accept our reality and embrace change is one step toward finding out what we need to do next in our life.

We become paralyzed rather than liberated by the power of choice. When we are presented with too many options, our brain doesn't know what to do with it all.

Research has shown that there is a sweet spot when it comes to choices. If we have too few, we feel limited. If we have too many, we feel overwhelmed.

How does this translate to your everyday life? If you're changing career fields and aren't sure what to switch over to, limit your options to five or six possible areas. Choose to mark one off the list every few days once you've sat with the choices a bit. As your brain focuses on fewer and fewer choices, it will become easier to see the direction you genuinely want to go in.

3. Take Small Steps With a 30-Day Challenge

In order to reprogram your conscious mind and stop saying "I don't know what to do with my life," set yourself a 30-day challenge.

You may ask, why 30 days? Because this is how the small steps you take gradually become your powerful habits

Setting a deadline has a powerful effect on motivation. Research has shown time and again that deadlines, even those that are self-imposed, can reduce procrastination and lead to better decision making.

Try setting one to three goals to be achieved during your 30-day challenge. Maybe you want to learn to code. Set weekly goals related to free online courses, and by the end of the month you'll have a good deal of knowledge under your belt.

Or perhaps you want to spend more time with your kids. Make a goal to have one family night each week where you offer all of your attention to your kids. You can even let them help plan what you will do on that special night.

Achieving these goals after one month will give you the confidence and self belief to keep going. It also helps you avoid doing nothing while you're feeling stuck. Once you know you can achieve one goal, you'll go on to achieve more and more.

Chapter 29:

How To Stop Being Lazy

How can I stop laziness?" The answer may not be as cut and dry as you'd expect. While some people may be more prone to being lazy than others, even highly productive people can find it challenging to get things done sometimes.

Here are some tips to help you get rid of laziness and get a grasp on your productivity.

Make Your Goals Manageable

Setting unrealistic goals and taking on too much can lead to burnout. While not an actual clinical diagnosis, the symptoms of burnout are recognized by medical professionals. Job burnout can cause exhaustion, loss of interest and motivation, and a longing to escape. Avoid overloading by setting smaller, attainable goals that will get you where you want to be without overwhelming you along the way.

Don't Expect Yourself To Be Perfect

Perfectionism is on the rise and it's taking a psychological toll. One 2017 study that looked at college students between 1989 and 2016 found an increase in perfectionism over the years. Researchers noted "young people [are] now facing more competitive environments, more unrealistic expectations, and more anxious and controlling parents than generations before." This rise in perfectionism is causing people to be overly critical of themselves and others. It's also led to an increase in depression and anxiety. Another smaller study of college students concluded that expecting perfection was related to avoidant coping, which causes you to avoid dealing with stressors.

Use Positive Instead Of Negative Self-Talk

Negative self-talk can derail your efforts to get things done in every aspect of your life. Telling yourself that you're a lazy person is a form of negative self-talk. You can stop your negative internal voice by practicing positive self-talk. Instead of saying, "There's no way I can get this done," say, "I'll give it my all to make it happen."

Create A Plan Of Action

Planning how you will get something done can make it easier to get there. Be realistic about how much time, effort, and other factors are needed to meet your goal and create an action plan. Having a plan will provide direction and confidence that can help even if you hit a hurdle along the way.

Use Your Strengths

Take a moment to think about what your strengths are when setting goals or gearing up to tackle a task. Try to apply them to different aspects of a task to help you get things done. Research has shown that focusing on strengths increases productivity, positive feelings, and engagement in work.

Recognize Your Accomplishments Along The Way

Patting yourself on the back for a job well done can help motivate you to keep going. Consider writing down all of your accomplishments along the way in everything you do, whether at work or home. It's a great way to boost your confidence and positivity, and fuel you to carry on.

Ask For Help

Many people believe that asking for help is a sign of weakness. But not asking for help could be setting you up for failure. A 2018 study found that people who don't ask co-workers for help were more likely to be dissatisfied in their jobs and had lower levels of job performance. They were also perceived less favourably by their employers. Asking for help improves your chances of success and helps you connect with others who can encourage and motivate you.

Avoid Distraction

We all have our favourite distractions we turn to when we're just not feeling like doing a task — whether it's scrolling through social media or playing with a pet. Find ways to make your distractions less accessible. This can mean finding a quiet place to work, like the library or an empty room, or using an app to block sites that you scroll mindlessly when you should be on task.

Reward Yourself

Getting a job done is a reward in itself, but some people are driven by external rewards. Focus on what you'll gain from getting something done, like getting closer to a promotion, or reward yourself for a job well done. Celebrate the end of a big project with a night out or invite friends over for drink after a day of cleaning.

Chapter 30:

Living Life Without Regrets

As Mick Jagger once said, "the past is a great place and I don't want to erase it or to regret it, but I don't want to be its prisoner either." Regret is like an uninvited ghost, and it likes to make an appearance when we are at our lowest. It dwells in the back of our heads from time to time and reminds us of the things that we wish we had done differently in our lives. But, just like a million other things and emotions, regrets only stay with us if we feed on it and let it in. It can be A heavy burden for us to carry, so in order to get rid of this lingering ghost, it's essential that we first understand what we are actually regretting and why.

If your life were about to end tomorrow - if that drunk doesn't stop at the red light, or the meteor is headed right for your house, would you go into your memory and start seeing your regrets? Or would you just accept it all and wish that you had lived your life more freely? Trust me when I say this, it's really okay to screw up. We're not people who can't make any mistakes and be flawless. Take A hurdler in the Olympics as an example; he knocks over about half of the hurdles in that 110 meters, and they don't even break stride. Because at the end, it's not about not knocking over any hurdles or running the perfect race, it all comes down to getting across the line. So don't ever fear or regret failing - you give it A shot, and that's all that matters in the end.

We all know how Michael Jordan struggled with his career. In his own words, "I've missed more than 9000 shots in my career. I've lost almost 3000 games. 26 times, I've been trusted to take the game winning shot and missed. I've failed over and over and over again in my life. And that's why I succeed." Had he given up in his first try, the world would have never known A legend like him. He must've had A thousand second thoughts every time he failed, he must've regretted opting basketball every time he lost A game, but he kept going and never gave up. We should have A similar outlook on our lives. No matter what we did in our past, or whatever our decisions were that led to what we are now, it all must have A connection or A meaning. We just have to stop, think, and analyze.

Now, the first step to explore the space of your mind and begin addressing the things that you regret, is to have A conversation with yourself. But keep in mind, this isn't A blame game and it definitely isn't meant for you to slip down into A rabbit hole of self-sabotage. Holding onto regret is one form of self-sabotaging, but you should move forward by identifying things that are working against you and having healthier conversations with yourself to get to the root of things. Regret is A powerful emotion, it can consume your thoughts, energy, and time. Feeling miserable is totally fine as long as you keep A check on yourself and don't let it drain you completely. No matter what your situation is, you can work on this "ghost of regret" to leave by starting doing positive things for yourself. Feed your life with passion and love, and regrets will say good-bye to you soon.

Chapter 31:

How To Stop Caring What People Think Of You

The Image On The Mirror

The mirror supposedly shows us exactly how we appear. We see what we believe to be us on it and we ask no questions. Well, at least we know that the mirror can be honest. Can the same be said about what people think of us? Most people are driven by their selfish ambitions. They cannot indeed be fair to you without putting their interests first. A time is coming when you have to be independent of what they think or say about you. This is because people can sometimes be oppressive in their thoughts toward you especially if there is nothing in it for them.

The Different Versions Of The Truth

The truth often depends on where you are standing. You could be on top of a hill or in a valley. Better yet, you could have locked yourself up in your house. All these circumstances inform why people could have different thoughts toward you. The most beautiful part in all this is that the truth shall remain unchanged and their thoughts toward you continue remaining insignificant. The time has come for you to gain your independence from other people and not care anymore what they think of you.

True Independence

Independence begins with oneself before it spreads elsewhere. The fact is that not everyone loves you or wishes you well. There will always be a few people who will not like you for no reason no matter how much you try to appease them. The effort you have put to change how they think toward you should transit to not caring about them anymore.

Here is how you can do it:

1. Trust In Your Abilities

Self-confidence is important if you want to achieve true independence. You have to believe in yourself first before others do. Continually seeking the validation of other people will make you indebted to them. A colonized mindset develops slowly even without you knowing and by the time you realize that things are getting out of hand, it could be too late to make an about-turn. Begin to trust in yourself as early as possible and build the capacity to be a self-made master. Instead of you seeking the validation of other people, they will be the ones seeking to be identified with you. That is how you turn the tables in your favor.

2. Believe In Systems, Not Personalities

People can never be institutions, no matter how strong their character is. They may tip toward one side because everyone has their biases (at least a majority of people do). Indeed, institutions are managed by people but what is reassuring is that they do not own them. They are simply agents put there at that particular time and their tenure shall end. Other people shall continue from where they left. Put your trust in institutions because they are governed by procedures and are not at the whims of individual interests. This upgrade in your thinking will move you toward true independence. You will no longer care about how what people think of you.

3. Stick To Your Plan

First of all, it is mandatory to have a plan. Haven't you heard that a good plan is a job half done? Following your plan to the latter denies you a chance to sway by popular opinion. Be ruthless when it comes to following your plan because it will embolden you to develop self-belief. People will discuss you and your newly-found attitude but your eyes must never leave the original plan because your goose is cooked once they do. Another thing that a plan does is to make you develop a thick skin. The words and actions of naysayers should not enter your head because they will make you trash your plan, the original one that was crafted by a winning spirit.

4. Change Your Company

The people you hang around with are very important because they determine the kind of person you become. If you keep the company of people who have their ears on roadside gossip, then you will become like them. If you also have strong-minded people as friends, you shall be strong-willed as they are. When you are about to backslide to your previous ways, your new friends will make you stop it. The secret to never turning back on your new resolve of not caring what people think is to change your company.

Conclusion

The journey to true independence is a long one but you must not give up. Once you break free from being chained by the thoughts of other people toward you, you bagged a gold medal!